Chess ASAP!

Chess
ASAP!

AVERY CARDOZA

CARDOZA PUBLISHING

Cardoza Publishing is the foremost gaming publisher in the world with a library of more than 200 up-to-date and easy-to-read books and strategies. These authoritative works are written by the top experts in their fields and with more than 10,000,000 books in print, represent the best-selling and most popular gaming books anywhere.

Library of Congress Catalog Card No: 2017964680
ISBN 13: 978-1-58042-369-5

Visit our website or write for a full list of Cardoza Publishing books and advanced strategies.

CARDOZA PUBLISHING
P.O. Box 98115, Las Vegas, NV 89193
Toll-Free Phone (800)577-WINS
email: cardozabooks@aol.com
www.cardozabooks.com

ABOUT THE AUTHOR

Avery Cardoza, a New York City high school team chess champion and a speed chess "monster," is a million-selling author of over 50 how-to gaming books. He is the founder of Cardoza Publishing, whose popular line of chess books have sold more than five hundred thousand copies worldwide.

TABLE OF CONTENTS

1. INTRODUCTION

I'm going to show you how to play and win at chess in just one reading! You'll learn to see the game with all its wonders and possibilities, armed with a confidence and set of skills that will separate you from other players new to the game.

You'll not only learn how the pieces move and their relative values, but also the strategies and tactics that lead to gaining an advantage over your opponent and, ultimately, winning games. I'll show you the best opening moves and why they're the correct plays to make, and how to avoid the bad opening moves that lead to losing positions. You'll also learn the various tactics and traps to capture your opponent's pieces, as well as the various checkmating combinations you'll need to see the game through to your final victory.

Fifteen power-packed chapters cover everything you need to know to build a strong foundation as a chess player and to have loads of fun in the game. From reading and writing chess notation (it's easy!), to playing a fun variant called speed chess, to competing in tournaments for cash and prizes and becoming a rated chess player—it's all here!

Chess is a fantastic game of skill enjoyed by millions of players around the world and you too can join in the challenge. There is a lot to learn and no time to waste.

Ready to play? Great—let's get to it now!

2. THE BASICS OF PLAY

Chess is played with two players, one competing against the other. One player takes the White pieces, though in actuality, the pieces are really off-white, or if made of wood, more of a blond color, and the other takes the Black pieces, which when made of wood, are typically more of a medium to dark brown color. In either case, the actual color of the pieces is not so important as that one plays "White" and the other "Black."

In this book, and in all writing on chess, whether in books, articles, or game compilations, the pieces will always be referred to as Black and White.

Two opponents sit across from one another with a chessboard and chess pieces between them, and alternate turns with White going first, followed by Black, and then by White again, and so on. Each player must take a turn and make one move before it is the next player's turn. You cannot skip a turn, nor can you make two moves in a row. Each player must make one move and one only before it is his opponent's turn.

White has the advantage because it moves first, giving it the opportunity to direct the initial tempo of the game. Of course, Black has a say in that as well because Black will make a move that puts his own mark on the flow of the game, but it is White with the initial play. Other than the edge White has in going first, there is no difference between playing White and playing Black. Their pieces start across from one another in identical formations and play according to the same rules.

OBJECT OF THE GAME

The goal in chess is to capture your opponent's king and when you do so, the game is over and you win. The fatal blow can occur as quickly as just a few minutes into a game between beginning players, and for advanced players locked in a deep battle, especially in a tournament, as much as five hours or longer. The average game length among novices, however, tends to run between thirty minutes and an hour and I'll show you a super fun variation of chess, which gives each player only five minutes total!

In a little bit, we'll see exactly how you accomplish capturing your opponent's king, but first let's get a better understanding of how the game works.

Let's start by taking a look at the board and the pieces.

THE CHESSBOARD

Chess is played on a square board of eight columns and eight rows, comprising a total of 64 alternating black and white squares, 32 of which are black squares and 32 white squares. Again, as with the pieces, black and white may not literally be "black and white," but dark squares and light squares. In fact, in roll-up boards often used in tournaments (and home play) the black squares are dark green and the white squares are off-white.

As with the pieces, the actual color of the board's squares are irrelevant.

THE PIECES

Each player starts with sixteen pieces—eight pawns, two each of knights, bishops and rooks, along with one queen and one king.

	Symbol		Each Player
Pawns	♙	♟	8
Knights	♘	♞	2
Bishops	♗	♝	2
Rooks	♖	♜	2
Queen	♕	♛	1
King	♔	♚	1

Total Pieces   **16 for White**
                                              16 for Black

Let's set up the pieces up on the board, before either player has made a move.

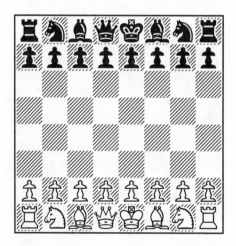

Starting position in chess

The eight pawns are lined up in a row and behind them, the more valuable pieces sit—the knights, bishops, rooks, queen, and king.

When setting up a board for play, there are two things to keep in mind:

1. A white square should always be in your right corner.

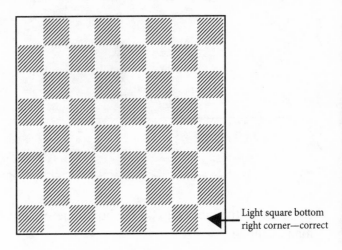

Light square bottom right corner—correct

Correct orientation of chessboard

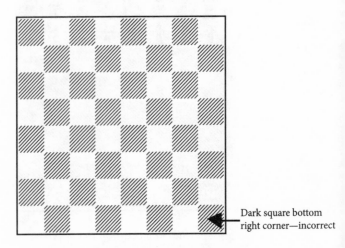

Dark square bottom right corner—incorrect

Incorrect orientation of chessboard

2. Queen should always be "on color," that is the White queen should start on a white square and the Black queen should start on a black square.

Correct orientation of king and queen

Incorrect orientation of king and queen

Now that we have the pieces and board set up correctly, it's time to see what the chess pieces at your disposal can do.

3. INTRODUCTION TO THE CHESS PIECES

In this chapter, you'll learn how the chess pieces move and capture along with their relative strengths so you get a sense of how the various pieces compare to one another in the game.

Pieces may move to any square on the board according to the movement ability for that piece, however, a piece may not move to any square already occupied by one of its own pieces. For example, a Black piece may not move to a square already occupied by another Black piece. On the other hand, a piece may move to a square occupied by an opponent's piece.

What happens if you land on a square occupied by an opponent?

Well, in that case you *capture* that piece and take it out of play. As a chess game progresses, you'll capture some of your opponent's pieces and he'll capture some of yours. When you capture a chess piece, that piece gets removed from the board and will be out of play for the remainder of the game.

Though the term "capture" is uniformly used in chess to describe pieces that are taken and removed from the board, a more appropriate term might be "killed" or "eliminated" since the piece gets permanently removed from the game and cannot reenter.

As you'll see later, if you get more of your opponent's pieces than he gets of yours, you have a big advantage that could lead to victory.

Let's now see how the chess pieces move and capture. We'll start with the weakest piece, the pawn, and work our way up to the most valuable piece, the king.

PAWNS

Pawns play important roles in chess, not only in creating strong defensive barriers and shielding the king from attack, but as weapons that, when working together, can create strong formations, and pressure an opponent's more powerful pieces. They're typically the first pieces to be moved, as well as captured, and they're usually in the heart of any action on the board.

Moving and Capturing With Pawns

A pawn can only move one square at a time in a forward direction—it cannot move backwards or sideways—except for the very first time it moves, when it may move forward one or two squares. On the first move of the game, all these moves, going forward only, are possible for White's pawns.

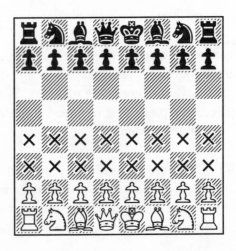

Possible opening pawn moves (forward movement only!)

In the following diagram, both Black and White have advanced their pawns forward two squares on their first moves. The "X" indicates the spots where White or Black, had they advanced only one square, could have moved their pawns as well.

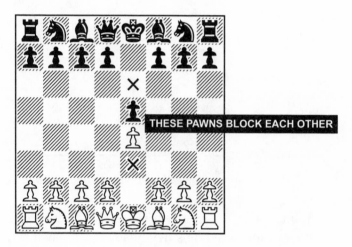

Pawns can move one or two squares on their first move

A pawn may continue to move forward one square at a time if the square directly in front of it is unoccupied. However, if another piece occupies the space in front of a pawn, the pawn is blocked and may not move forward. In the diagram above, the central pawns are blocking one another and cannot advance further.

Pawns, however, can move one square forward on a *diagonal* when they're capturing an opponent's piece. Unlike the other pieces, which move and capture in the same manner, pawns move differently than they capture.

In the following diagram, on White's second turn, he has moved the pawn in front of his queen forward two squares.

Let's see what this looks like.

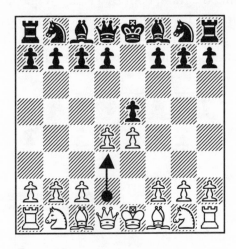

White moves his queen pawn up two squares

While Black's king pawn is unable to move directly forward, it can capture White's newly advanced pawn since it is on the neighboring diagonal—and indeed he does.

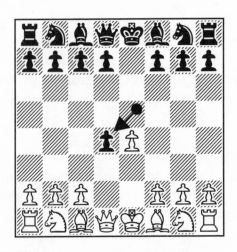

Black's pawn captures White's pawn

Value of Pawns

Pawns are the lowliest of the chess pieces, worth the least but they're not to be ignored as insignificant. The deeper into a game one goes, the more valuable pawns become because they have a magical quality to them—if pushed all the way down, they can transform into the mightiest piece on the board. We will look at this "magical" quality later, in the chapter "Special Chess Moves."

However, if one has to sacrifice or lose any piece on the board, you'll almost always want it to be the pawn since it has the least relative value. Anytime you can trade a pawn for a more powerful piece—knight, bishop, rook, or queen—with all else equal, you have gained an advantage over your opponent.

During a game, you'll look for every opportunity to trade a pawn for a piece of greater value.

KNIGHTS

The knights play an important role in the opening, both in attacking the opponent's central pawns and defending their own. They tend to be the first major pieces developed because of their ease in getting into play and their unique ability to move.

Moving and Capturing With Knights

The knight is the only piece on the board that can jump over other pieces. As opposed to other non-pawn pieces, the knight doesn't need pawns to clear a path for its first move. It just pops over the pawns and gets right into the action.

The knight moves in an L shape, two squares in any direction and then, perpendicularly, one square to the side—forming the letter "L." Or, you can think of it in the opposite manner, one square in any direction and two squares, perpendicularly, to the side.

In the following diagram, the knight makes its L-shaped move on White's second turn, jumping over pawns to enter the game. The knight has moved into an attacking position and threatens Black's central pawn. The "X" indicates the empty squares the knight could also move to on its subsequent turn, in addition to taking off Black's central pawn.

Black answers with a corresponding knight move as well, jumping over his own pieces to enter the fray.

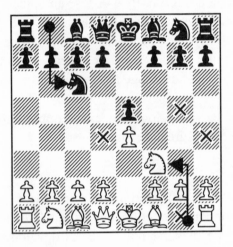

White's knight jumps into action. Black's does as well.

In the next diagram, we see White make an ill-advised capture of Black's central pawn.

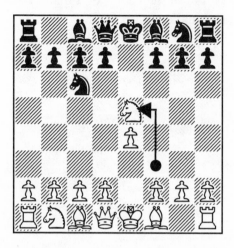

White's knight capture's Black's central pawn

It was ill advised because Black's knight then takes off White's knight, a bad exchange for White, who only received a pawn in return.

Here is the position after Black's capture of White's knight.

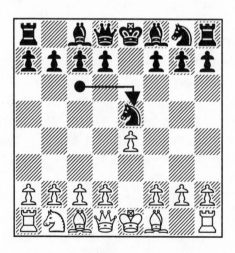

Black's knight capture's White's knight, winning the exchange

I've placed a knight in the center of a blank board. It can land on all the squares marked with an "X."

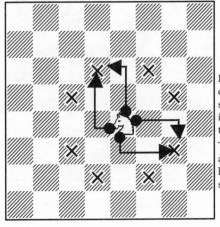

Either two spaces in one direction, and one sideways; or one space in one direction and two sideways.

There are two ways to arrive at each of the highlighted squares, shown with the arrows.

The knight can reach all the squares marked with an "X"

If a knight lands on a square occupied by an opponent's piece, it captures that piece, and the captured piece gets removed from the board. Like all other pieces, the knight may not land on a square occupied by another piece of its own color.

Value of Knights

Knights are equivalent in value to bishops, more valuable than pawns, but not as important as a rook or queen. In other words, it is okay to exchange a knight for another knight or a bishop, but bad to exchange one for a pawn. If you can somehow trade a knight for a rook, you've gained a nice advantage over your opponent, but if you lose it only to gain a pawn, that puts you at a disadvantage.

BISHOPS

You start with one white bishop and one black bishop. The "white" and "black" designation of bishops refer to the squares the bishop patrols—the white bishop will remain on the white squares throughout the entire game and the black bishop remains on the black squares—not the bishop belonging to the White or Black player. (Note the lower case "white" and "black," for the color of the square or piece, as opposed to the upper case, "White" and "Black," designating the color of the players.)

Moving and Capturing With Bishops

Bishops move along the diagonals as far as the open squares allow. They may traverse the board forwards or backwards along the black or white diagonal they started the game on, but may not pass through or jump over pieces. Bishops capture any opponent's piece occupying a square they land on, but of course, may not land on a square occupied by their own piece.

In the beginning, bishops can't go anywhere, as they're trapped behind their own pawns. But once the pawns blocking their path open a pathway, they have room to operate and become more valuable as a weapon in your chess arsenal.

After White's king pawn advances, the bishop is no longer stuck. It can move to the five squares marked below.

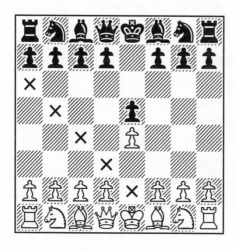

Once the pawn advances, the bishop can reach these squares

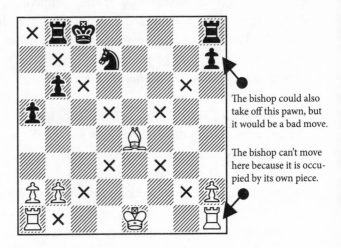

The bishop could also take off this pawn, but it would be a bad move.

The bishop can't move here because it is occupied by its own piece.

The bishop can move to any of the squares marked with an "X"

The above endgame position shows the full range of a bishop. From this position in the center of the board, the bishop can reach the eleven squares marked with an "X," plus the highlighted pawn in the upper corner area of the board, though that would be a bad move because Black would capture right back with his rook, winning the exchange. The bishop cannot move to the lower right-hand corner because it is occupied by its own piece, a White rook.

Value of Bishops

Bishops are more valuable than pawns because of their range. They have the equivalent value of a knight, but are not as valuable as a rook or a queen, both of which have greater mobility and therefore are more powerful pieces. Trading a bishop for an opponent's bishop or knight is an equal trade. However, if you can grab a rook for that same bishop you've come out ahead. If you manage to exchange a queen for your bishop, you have a huge advantage that with solid play should lead to an easy win.

ROOKS

In the beginning of a game, rooks are ineffective because they're trapped in the corners of the board. As the game develops and the rooks free up—maybe one through castling and the other through natural development—they become important strategic pieces. If they're still around in the endgame, their range and importance gets even more prominent.

Moving and Capturing With Rooks

Rooks move in a straight line, along the ranks and files, backwards and forwards, left and right, for as far as the open squares permit. It cannot jump over pieces like a knight or bypass pieces blocking its path. If an opposing piece is on a square the rook wishes to land on, the rook can capture that piece and remove it from the board. If the piece is of the same color, in other words, it is on the same team, the rook may not move to that square.

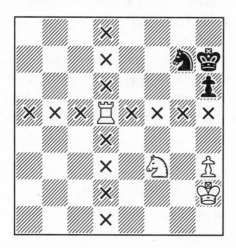

The rook can move to any of these squares

In the diagram above, the mobility of the rook is revealed in this endgame position.

Value of Rooks

Rooks are the most powerful piece on the board outside of the queen. You don't want to voluntarily exchange a rook for a knight or a bishop—those pieces are less valuable and you would lose the exchange. You also wouldn't want to exchange them for just a pawn, which would be a catastrophic exchange for a rook. However, if you could capture an opponent's queen and lose just a rook, that would give you a tremendous advantage which should lead to victory.

QUEEN

The queen is the most powerful chess piece because it has the greatest range of all the pieces. Because of its great power, it is the second most important piece in the game, right behind the king who's safety, of course, is of paramount importance.

Moving and Capturing With the Queen

The queen moves like a bishop or a rook, in other words, it can go along any diagonal, rank or file as long as the path is unobstructed. It captures by landing on a square occupied by the enemy, and removes the slain piece from the board. As with the other chess pieces, you cannot move your queen onto a square already occupied by your own piece, nor can the queen jump like a knight.

Thus, on the first move of the game, the queen is blocked behind its own pawns, but once a central pawns advances, the queen can come out and play.

Let's see just how mobile the queen is.

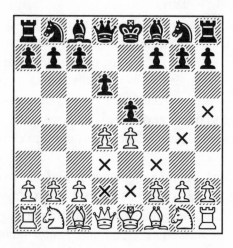

After two opening pawn moves—freedom!

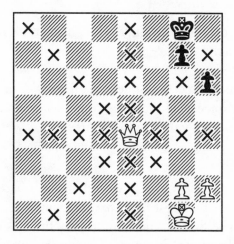

The queen has tremendous range in this endgame!

In the first diagram, after a few opening pawn moves, the queen's range has expanded to these six squares. In the second diagram, well into the endgame, the queen's range is twenty-five squares in this open board!

Value of the Queen

You don't exchange your queen for any other piece unless it is another queen. Anything less—a knight, bishop, rook, or a lowly pawn—would be a terrible exchange, in fact, a catastrophic one. The queen is so valuable that if it was traded off for any lesser piece, it would be too much of a loss to overcome between good players, and the player losing the queen would resign on the spot. There would be no point in continuing.

Among beginners anything can happen and you would fight this battle to the end, but you won't find any good player continuing the battle short an uncompensated queen unless he had a mate in the works, a tremendous positional advantage that would lead to mate, or enough compensation from captured knights, bishops or rooks, as to render the exchange even.

But a queen behind with only a knight or rook in exchange? No—game over.

In other words, protect your queen at all costs! You should avoid moving your queen out too early in the game unless you need to, because it is too valuable to risk its loss, as we'll see later.

KING

The king is not the most powerful piece—that piece is the queen—but it is the most *important* one and must be protected at all costs. The loss of your king means the loss of the game. On the other hand, if you can capture your opponent's king, you win.

Moving and Capturing With the King

The king can move backwards, forwards, or diagonally in any direction—but just one square at a time. In other words, it can move to any adjoining square as long as one its own pieces do not occupy the square and that square is not under attack by an opposing piece. In the beginning of the game, like all the non-pawn pieces except the knight, the king is unable to go anywhere since it is hemmed in by its own pieces.

In the diagram below, after the pawn advances, the king is free to move forward one square (marked by an "X"). However, that would be about the worst possible move White could make.

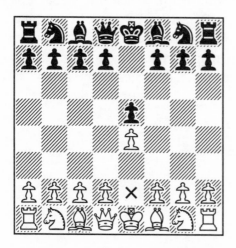

The king is freed up for one move, though it would be a terrible move

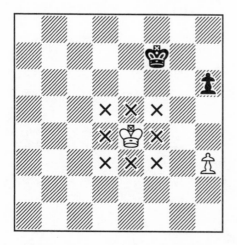

The king can move to any adjoining square

In the previous diagram, an endgame situation, you see the king's full range on this open board.

Value of the King

In the beginning of the game, the king is a quiet piece with a limited role. One of your early goals, while positioning your pieces into good attacking and defensive formations, is to protect the king from harm. When the endgame is reached (if a game goes that far), with few pieces remaining on the board, the king becomes an important offensive weapon, protecting pawns and helping shepherd them down the board to greater glory. We'll see that that means later when we talk about *pawn promotion*.

4. CHECKMATE, CHECK, & DRAWN GAMES

In this chapter we'll go over the basic plays of checking and checkmating, plus situations in which neither player wins—that is, draws and stalemates.

CHECKMATE

The object of chess is to attack the opposing king such that it cannot defend itself or escape, called *checkmate* or simply, *mate*. Checkmate ends the game with the player delivering checkmate being the winner. In the diagram below, Black used his queen and rook together to trap his opponent's king. White's king has no escape square that clears it of the attacking piece's range, thus it's checkmate.

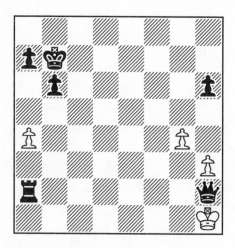

Queen and rook checkmate

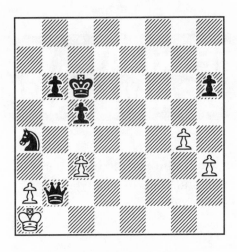

Queen and knight checkmate

In the above diagram, Black's knight-and-queen combination work in unison for the fatal checkmate.

In both checkmates, Black's attacking queen cannot be captured by White's king because the queens are protected by its own pieces—in the first diagram, by the rook, and in the second diagram, by the knight. In other words, the king cannot take off Black's queen because the supporting piece would be able to capture it right back.

However, if the queen was *not* supported by another piece, that is, no piece was protecting it, then the king could simply land on the queen's square and capture it!

We have a chapter later on dedicated to strategies for checkmating your opponent's king where we'll take a closer look at different ways to achieve this.

But what if the king *can* escape? Aha! Let's look at that now.

CHECK

When the king falls under attack—in other words, an opposing piece is capable of taking a king off the board on the next move—but it is not trapped and can escape, then he is in *check*. For example, in the following diagram, White's bishop has moved and put the Black king into check.

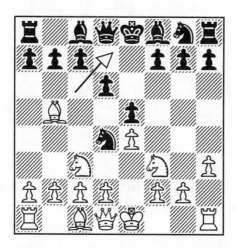

White's bishop checks Black's king

By the rules of chess, the king must *immediately* get out of check. Even if a player has an incredible move which would capture his opponent's queen or checkmate the king, those moves cannot be made if his own king is in check. A player's king must be brought to safety, that is, out of check, before any other moves are made.

There are three way's to get out of check. Using the above position, we will show the three possibilities.

1. The king may simply move out of check. In the diagram below, Black's king moved forward one square.

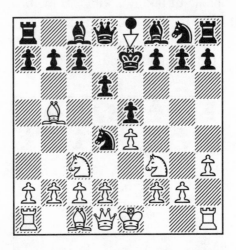

2. The check may be intercepted by a piece that blocks the checking piece's path. In the diagram below, Black's bishop moved diagonally one square, blocking the check and attacking the White bishop giving the check. (If White takes the bishop, Black can capture back with his queen or king.)

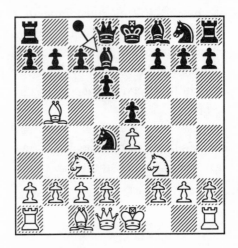

3. A piece can capture the attacker and remove the threat.

In this position, Black's knight captures White's bishop. (Of course, White would then capture back with his knight and stay even in material.)

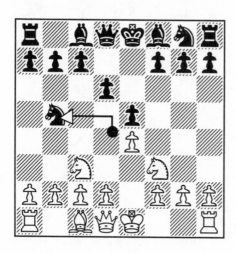

The King May Not Move into Check

The king is not allowed to move into check, that is, the king cannot move onto a square that is being attacked.

In the following diagram, the squares marked with an "X" are off limits for the king as he would be moving into check. Black's rook attacks the file next to the king and the bishop attacks the black square to the right diagonal of the king.

If, for some reason, you wanted to move the king in this position, the white square in the corner would be the only move allowed.

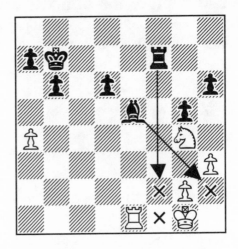

The king may not move to the squares marked with an x.

RESIGNATION

There is an additional way besides checkmate to win a chess game and that is when your opponent **resigns**. Resignation is common in games among intermediate or advanced players when one side's advantage over the other is so great that the end result is pretty much a foregone conclusion; in other words, the losing player has a negligent chance of winning. For top players, a resignation could be triggered by the loss of a knight or bishop or even the loss, in the endgame, of a single lowly pawn. Losing a major piece like a rook or queen would be too difficult to overcome and would certainly lead to a resignation.

Resignation is typically signaled by the defeated player tipping over his king, a universal signal informing his opponent, "I resign, you win." This can also be expressed verbally.

Against novices, who are prone to **blunders** (terrible moves) and traps, games are never over until they're over and should be battled out until a checkmate is actually delivered.

Note that it is customary to shake your opponent's hand when he wins, whether by resignation, or checkmate.

DRAWS AND STALEMATES

There are situations in chess where neither side will emerge victorious. In these situations, the game will be considered a *draw*. There are six ways that a chess game can be drawn.

1. Impossible to Win

A game will be drawn when it is impossible for either player to win. Two such situations are when a king-and-bishop or king-and-knight combination face off against a lone king.

King and knight versus king is a draw

2. Perpetual Check

When one side can continually check an opponent and states his intention to do so—and the other side cannot prevent this—the game will be considered drawn.

3. Triple Repetition

When an exact set of moves are repeated on three full turns (Black and White moving three times each), the player whose turn is next may call a draw, and if that player repeats his move, than the other player may call the draw.

4. 50-Move Rule

If fifty turns go by without a single piece being captured by either player and no pawn has moved, either player may declare a draw.

5. Stalemate

A *stalemate* occurs when a player not in check has no possible play other than to move into check.

In the diagram below, it is White's turn and he has an overwhelming advantage. However, he blows the almost sure win by taking away Black's escape hatch. White's play, moving the rook as seen in the second diagram, was a terrible blunder. It is now Black's turn to move and he has no move except *into* check—that's a stalemate. (If, instead, White had slid his rook over one square to the left, it would have been checkmate.)

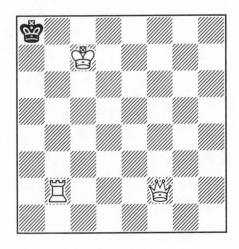

White to move

Stalemate! White's overwhelming advantage goes to waste

6. Agreement to Draw

There is one final drawn situation. This occurs when the players agree that neither will be able to checkmate the other and rather than playing out a game with little to no winning chances, they agree to the draw.

HOW QUICKLY CAN YOU CHECKMATE AN OPPONENT?

Pretty quickly, actually. A common beginner's checkmate can be made in just four moves. Players new to chess commonly fall for this mate. But there is a quicker mate, one that can only be delivered by Black, and it takes just two moves!

We'll look at both of these lightning-quick checkmates later.

5. SPECIAL CHESS MOVES

Chess has three special move rules and they all involve pawns.

CASTLING

Castling occurs when the king and rook, moving in unison, flip relative positions such that the king moves toward the greater safety of the corner and the rook frees up toward the center. There are two types of castling, *kingside castling*, on the king's short side (two empty squares between king and rook), and *queenside castling*, when the king crosses over the queen's original space (three empty squares between king and rook). Note the term, *empty spaces*—no pieces can be between the king and rook.

In the game below, after five moves, White and Black have prepared their pieces for castling and the board looks like this:

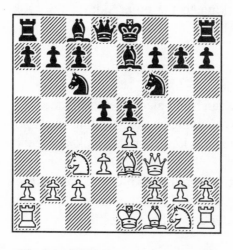

Black and White in position to castle

It is White's turn and he castles on the queenside. Black castle as well and does so on the kingside. The position after each side has castled:

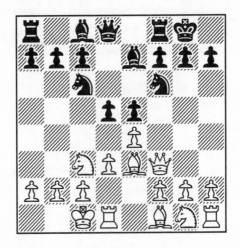

White after castling queenside; Black after castling kingside

Both sides have developed their pieces, protected their kings through castling, and have a nice start to the game. Here is an easy way to remember where the pieces end up after castling, whether kingside or queenside. Slide the rook next to the king, then flip the king to the other side of the rook, then *ouila*— you're castled!

Three conditions must be present for castling to occur:

1. There can be no pieces between the king and rook. Thus, when the game begins, castling is not possible.
2. Neither the king nor the rook can have moved previously.
3. The king cannot be in check, move into check, or pass through check. (A little known fact is that the rook can be under attack before castling.)

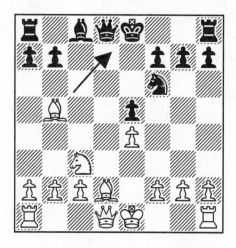

Black's king is in check—he cannot castle

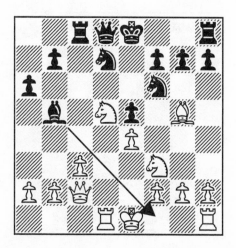

Black's bishop attacks a castling square—White cannot castle

In the first diagram, Black must remove the checking situation to castle, for example, blocking the check with his own bishop. Similarly, in the second diagram, the bishop's reach into White's castling area must be blocked in order to castle.

For example, White could push the pawn forward in front of the queen to block the bishop's path, or he can attack the bishop and force it to withdraw to a position where it can't attack the king's castling squares.

EN PASSANT

En passant is a special pawn capture that allows a pawn moving two squares forward on its very first move to be taken off by an opposing pawn as if it had moved only one square forward. Let's see what this looks like.

In the game position below, it is Black's turn and he moves his king pawn up two squares, situating it directly next to White's queen pawn.

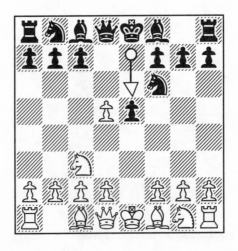

Black's king pawn advances two squares

White takes *en passant*. The position after White's *en passant* capture is shown in the following diagram.

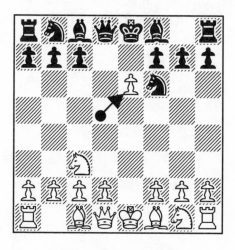

White takes en passant

Three conditions must be present for an *en passant* move:

1. A pawn advances forward two squares—which, of course, would be the very first move for that pawn in the game.
2. The advancing pawn lands directly to the left or right side of a square occupied by an opposing pawn.
3. The option to move *en passant* can only be exercised by the opposing player on his very next turn. Once that turn has passed, *en passant* is no longer possible.

PAWN PROMOTION

Pawn promotion occurs when a pawn advances all the way down to the last rank of the chessboard (or first rank, if looking at Black's perspective) and gets promoted to any piece of the player's choice, with the exception of a king or pawn. The ever-present threat of pawn promotion heavily influences endgame play as both sides battle furiously either to promote their pawns or stop the other side from promoting—all the while maneuvering for material superiority or a game-ending checkmate.

In the following diagram, it is White's turn. His pawn is on the seventh rank, one move way from promotion.

White to move

White's pawn advances to the very last rank and promotes to a queen! Unless White makes an absolutely terrible blunder, Black has a lost game.

White promotes his pawn to a queen

While you can promote the pawn to a knight, bishop, rook, or queen, you'll almost always choose the queen because it is the most powerful piece. There are a few occasions where you might choose a different piece, either to avoid a rare stalemate situation, or when a promotion to a knight actually delivers a checkmate (also rare).

What if you already have a queen? Well, now you have two of them! Players will usually turn a captured rook upside down to indicate that it is a queen, so it won't be confused with a rook. You could even get a third queen, or more, but that would be silly, since two queens is more than enough to crush your opponent.

TOUCH RULE AND J'ADOUBE

In tournaments, chess is played with the "touch" rule—if you touch a piece, you have to move it. For example, in a tournament, if you touch your knight, but decide instead that you want to move your bishop, it is too late, you have already committed to moving the knight. And once you remove your hand from a piece after placing it on a square, that move is considered finished and your turn over. You can't take the move back, no matter how disastrous that move may be.

At beginning levels, players are always touching pieces and changing their minds. This is a bad habit you should try to break. Learn to think with your brain and not your fingers!

You can touch a piece without being committed to moving it, but only if you announced your intention first. The common declaration for this is *j'adoube*, French for "I adjust." For example, if a piece was positioned on the edge of a square or at an odd angle to the point where it is annoying, you simply announce, *j'adoube*, and then you are free to adjust the piece without being committed to moving it.

Now that we have a handle on all the pieces, how they move, how they capture and their relative values, let's see how chess games are recorded.

6. EASY CHESS NOTATION

Wait right there—don't get intimidated and don't run! Keep the book right in front of you. The word "notation" sounds intimidating, but really, chess notation is not hard to learn. In fact, you'll know how to write and read chess moves in no time at all. I promise! That is, you'll be able to record your own chess games for eternity, or replay games by yourself, your friends, or the greatest players of all time, champions like Bobby Fisher, Garry Kasparov, Hideki Nakamura, Magnus Carlsen, and many other all-time great chess players.

We need the language of chess notation to help us easily describe the strategies and moves in a chess game as we'll do in this book. You'll see that done in just about every chess book or article about the game.

Let's get to it!

RANKS AND FILES

The chess board is described in a grid, with the numbers, 1 to 8 for the rows running horizontally, left to right, called *ranks*, and the letters a to h for the columns, called *files*, running vertically, 1 being on White's back rank and 8, being on Black's back rank.

White's starting pieces are always shown on the bottom in chess diagrams on rank's 1 and 2, and Black's starting pieces on ranks 7 and 8, as you see in the following diagram.

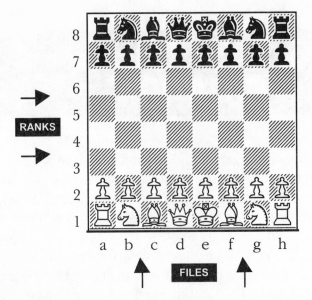

Boards are always displayed from White's perspective, with the White pieces at the bottom and the Black ones at the top.

CHESS PIECE SYMBOLS

Each major piece is described by a letter, as follows:

Pawn*	
Bishop	B
Knight	N
Rook	R
Queen	Q
King	K

Well, that's easy enough, right?

Each piece is represented by the first letter of its spelling, except the knight, where the silent "K" is dropped (since it duplicates the king) and "N" is used instead. I know, I know— the space for the pawns is left blank. Good catch! With pawns, chess notation doesn't use the letter "P"; instead the square the pawn moves to is referenced (no letter is used), for example, h4 describes a pawn moving to the h4 square. What we'll do next is show the piece that is moving and the square it is moving to. Here are what some moves might look like.

d5   Describes a pawn moving to d5
Qh4   Describes the queen going to the h4 square
Rc8   Describes a rook going to the c8 square

Other Notation Symbols Used

Capturing   x
Castling   0-0   kingside
Castling   0-0-0   queenside

Capturing will be described by a small "x." For example, if a knight takes a piece on the g5 square, the notation will read Nxg5. Notation doesn't describe what was on the g5 square, since only one piece can be there. In the context of a game, only one capture on that square is possible so the action is clear.

When a pawn captures, you'll show the file it captured from and list it in *lower case*, for example, exg5, describes the pawn on the e-file taking the piece on the g5 square. The letters for pawn captures are always listed in lower case (a, b, c, d, e, f, g, h to describe the files), as opposed to the upper case treatment for the other pieces (N, B, R, Q, K), such as Rxd1 (rook takes the piece on the d1 square).

If it had been a queen that captured in the situation above, it would have read Qxd1 as opposed to Rxd1.

Let's play out the beginning of a game and record the moves as we go along so you get comfortable with the notation. White moves will be shown on the left and Black on the right. White goes first, moving the pawn in front of his king two spaces and Black responds with the same move.

White	**Black**
1. e4	e5

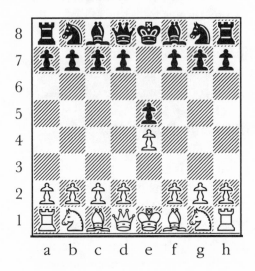

White brings out a knight on the kingside and again Black mimics the move on the other side of the board.

2. Nf3	**Nc6**

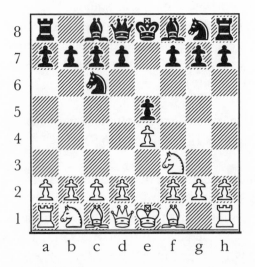

White moves up his queen pawn two spaces and Black pushes his queen pawn up one space to help defend his king pawn.

3. d4   **d6**

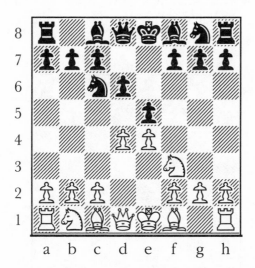

4. Bb5

White advances his bishop to the b5 square.

Now the fireworks begin.

4...   **exd4**

Black's e-pawn takes White's pawn at d4. Since it is a pawn capturing, the small letter is used, in this case, the "e," to signify that the e-pawn is capturing the piece on d4.

5. Nxd4

White captures back with his knight.

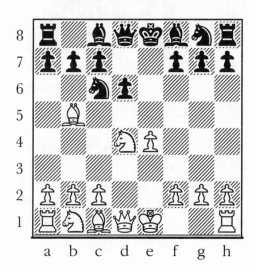

You see? Notation is not all that hard.

If you were reading about this game without the diagrams and without the moves listed in columns, which I have done to make this beginning notation easy to follow, it would look like this: **1. e4 e5; 2. Nf3 Nc6; 3. d4 d6; 4. Bb5 exd4; 5. Nxd4.**

The numbers indicate the moves in the game, for example "**1**" would be the first move, with a space separating White's move from Black's. So White went **1.e4** on his first move and Black moved **1…e5** (both pawn moves since the lower case was used), and then on to the second move "**2**" where White move his knight to f3 (**2.Nf3**) and Black responded with his own knight move to the c6 square (**2…Nc6**). And so on.

If there is commentary after a White move, when the game notation picks up again, Black's move will be preceded by three dots, for example, "Black needs to do something about the pin on his knight. **5…Bd7; 6. 0-0.**" (After Black moved his bishop to d7, White's sixth move was kingside castling, **6. 0-0.**)

SPECIAL NOTATION SITUATIONS
Two Pieces Can Capture on the Same Square

What if two rooks or two knights can capture or move to the same square? Then you need to describe which knight or rook is the capturing or moving piece. In these instances, you list the rank from which the piece originated after indicating the piece.

For example, if knights on the e- and h-files can both capture a piece on f4, you would write Nexf4 if the knight on the e-file captured the piece and Nhxf4 if instead it was the knight on the h-file. If both knights are on the same file, you would use the rank designation instead, for example, N6xc4, indicating the knight on the 6th rank made the capture.

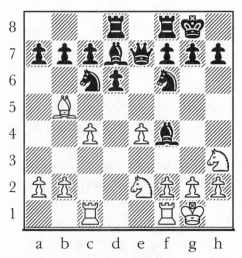

Nexf4 or Nhxf4 to describe either knight capturing the f4 bishop

Pawn Promotion

If the a-pawn advances all the way down to a queen you would indicate it as follows:

a8=Q. Or if, for example, to a knight: a8=N.

Check

When a king is in check, you add the "+" sign after the move, for example, **Bb5+.** This means, the bishop moved to the b5 square, putting the opposing king in check.

Checkmate

To notate a checkmate, you add the "#" sign after the move (or write "checkmate" or "mate"), for example, **Rd1#.**

Results Symbols

1-0 means White won
0-1 means Black won
½-½ indicates a draw

En Passant Capture

White has just moved 5.c4 and Black will capture en passant with his d4 pawn. It would be written like this: **dxc3 e.p.** or simply **dxc3** (the d-pawn takes the piece on c3—where the *en passant* pawn would be if it moved one square instead of two).

Commentary Symbols

!   An exceptionally good move

?   A blunder (bad move)

!!   An incredibly good move, one that pretty much seals a victory

??   A horrible blunder that pretty much leads to a loss

7. SEVEN PRINCIPLES OF WINNING CHESS

Bad chess players are bad chess players because they violate sound strategic principles of chess, that is, they make poor choices. However, there is no reason to make blatantly unsound moves because the principles of smart chess are easy to follow—all you have to do is implement them! If you stick to a few simple guidelines, your game will immediately be superior to the masses of novice chess players whose moves are just willy-nilly.

I have broken the game down to seven key principles. Add these into your game and your chess-playing future will have a solid strategic base to build on.

SEVEN IMPORTANT WINNING CONCEPTS
1. Develop Your Pieces
2. Attack the Center
3. Castle to Protect Your King
4. Only Trade Pieces of Equal Value or Better
5. Make the Best Move Available
6. Don't Wastefully Move Pieces Twice
7. Consider Why Your Opponent Made His Move

Let's go over these important concepts before we talk about specific moves. The first three concepts specifically apply to the opening of the game, the other four to the game as a whole.

1. DEVELOP YOUR PIECES

Beginning players move pieces into the wrong spots and take too long to get their pieces out into action. For example, you'll see players making too many pawn moves in lieu of getting their important pieces out on the board. This not only weakens their position, but leaves valuable knights and bishops stuck on the home ranks too long, their powers wasted on the back ranks.

Ignoring the cardinal rule for developing pieces leaves a player ripe for getting crushed by an opponent who has developed his pieces and lined them up into attacking formations.

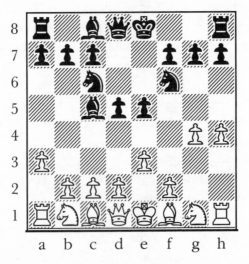

Too many pawn moves

In the above diagram, White has fallen in love with his pawns and all of his non-pawn pieces remain stuck in the back ranks. On the other side of the board, Black has developed his pieces and is ready to castle. Trouble is brewing and Black will soon be in control of this game. White has ignored the importance of the center, a topic we will touch on now…

2. ATTACK THE CENTER

The opening is a battle for control of the center. Your moves should contribute to that main battle, meaning they should put pressure on the central squares as opposed to the outer squares of the board. While we will cover this concept in depth in the following chapter, "The Opening: Good and Bad Moves," for now, the key idea to understand now is that you want to move your pieces toward the center, not away from it.

The diagram in the prior section showed Black doing just that while White's moves were random. Black had a big head start and thus, an advantage in that game.

3. CASTLE AND PROTECT YOUR KING

A common beginner's mistake is a failure to castle. Heck, you sometimes see that fundamental play ignored by good players. The price to pay for leaving a king unprotected in the middle is a king susceptible to attack and a game that could hang in the balance because of that. And yet the solution to this situation is so simple—castle!

There is an additional benefit to castling, one that takes on greater significance later in the game. Your rook goes from being trapped and useless in the corner to being an active weapon in the center. The process of castling forces you to make good moves anyway. Your pieces must get clear of the space between the king and the rook, meaning they get developed (hopefully, in the right way), a side benefit of castling.

Your goal in the opening is to develop pieces and get them out into the center where they can exert pressure on your opponent. When you follow those principles, your king will be perfectly positioned to castle and be in a relatively safe spot behind a wall of pawns.

4. ONLY TRADE PIECES OF EQUAL VALUE OR BETTER

Your pieces are like ordinance of an army heading into battle. If your weapons are superior, you have a big edge, and if they're vastly superior, an almost insurmountable edge. There is an old saying: Don't bring a knife to a gun battle. This concept applies to chess—if you're vastly outgunned, you're at a disadvantage that is very difficult to overcome against a good player.

We went over the relative value of pieces earlier. Let's review them again in order of greatest importance. Note, the king is not given a value because he is not a fungible commodity—he can't be lost without losing the game! The queen is by the most powerful piece, followed by the rook, then the bishop and knight, which are about of equal strength, and lastly, the pawn, which is the least powerful of all the pieces.

Anytime you can trade a piece of lesser value for a piece of greater value, you have enhanced your chances of winning. If you've captured a queen and lost any piece other than your own queen in the exchange, you have almost an insurmountable edge over your opponent. A rook traded for a pawn is also a disastrous loss, though less so than the queen. If you can trade a knight for a rook, or a pawn for a bishop, you have won those exchanges as well, and are in a superior position over your opponent, all other things being equal.

A point value system, universally used in chess, will help you get a sense of the individual values of chess pieces. Note that this is not the be all and end all of whether you're ahead or behind in the game—we will see many situations in this book where a material superiority loses to an underdog—but it will at least give you a sense of relative values of the pieces.

Chess Point Value System

Queen	9 points
Rook	5 points
Bishop	3 points
Knight	3 points
Pawn	1 point

Note that the actual value of a piece is dependent on the position and stage of the game—the values of pieces in the middle game might be different than in the endgame—and these point values should not be used as an exact guide. But they're useful, nonetheless, as a guide to comparing values of the pieces. For example, you'd be happy to trade a rook for your opponent's knight *and* bishop, and if you lost a knight, but gained three of your opponent's pawns in the process, you'd be okay too. (In the endgame, actually, you might have a big edge trading a knight for three pawns, depending on the other factors in play.)

5. MAKE THE BEST MOVE AVAILABLE

This advice is not as obvious or ridiculous as it first appears. Well, of course, you should always make the best play you can, but in the real world, that's not how it always works. In fact, knowingly making second-best moves is a common shortcoming among beginners.

Players can get into the bad habit of assuming their opponents will make weak moves. While it is not the worst assumption when you're playing unskilled opponents, it is a dangerous assumption to make and a bad habit to form. First, if your opponent doesn't make the bad move you expect, it has led *you* to make a bad move instead of the best move. Who is the fool here? Second, your goal should be to continually improve your game and to be the best player you can. Making poor choices of moves is not the way to achieve that.

There is an exception to attempting to make the best move and that occurs when you're so far behind, you need desperate measures to salvage a game headed for a loss. We cover that topic later, in the chapter, "Saving Lost Games."

Again, always assume your opponent will make a good move and proceed accordingly if you want to develop into the best player you can possibly be.

6. DON'T WASTEFULLY MOVE PIECES TWICE

It is an advantage to play White because you move first and get to set the tone of the game. Your opponent must react to your moves. It would be an even bigger advantage if you could move twice in a row. And while the rules don't allow that, poor play can effectively give a player an extra move or two (or three—see "Bad Queen Moves" later).

That's exactly what happens when you move a piece onto a square and then retreat it if subsequently gets attacked by your opponent. If your goal is to induce an opponent to weaken their position by such a move and you have a strong plan to exploit the situation, that is fine. But if, as is usually the case, you allow an opponent to push forward while you retreat to the same square in which you started, you've not only lost your initiative, but have allowed your opponent an extra free move or more—one for him to attack your prematurely placed piece while he's developing and a second move because it's now his turn!

The cure—think ahead. Consider how your opponent may react to your move. Which leads us to the next concept...

7. CONSIDER WHY YOUR OPPONENT MADE HIS MOVE

If you take just a few seconds to consider how your opponent's move affects the game and what he is trying to accomplish, you'll avoid blunders you otherwise might have made. Too often, a player becomes so fixated with his own plan of attack that he completely ignores the significance of his opponent's plan or prior move. This same type of tunnel vision happens to players in all types of competitions, from cash or tournament poker games to sports contests like football. And in all these competitions—as in life—it leads to missteps and disasters.

Allow a few seconds to consider the purpose of your opponent's play, that is, *think* before you move, and you may avoid bad plays such as the following:

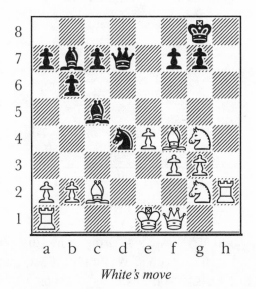

White's move

Black has just moved his knight from c6 to d4, but. White, enjoying the comfort of a two-piece advantage, doesn't think about Black's move—his eyes dazzle with the possibility of a great idea that he has been working on—he sees an opportunity to mate Black in just two moves. He just needs to move his queen to the h1-square so that it lines up with the rook on h2, and then shoot the h2 rook down to h8—checkmate.

17. Qh1. White moves forward with his plan, lining his queen up with the rook on the h-file. In just one more move, he'll deliver the decisive blow.

But he'll never get the chance.

17....Nxc2+. Black's knight moves again and takes the bishop on c3. Check!

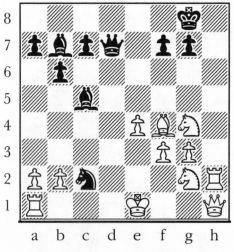

An unexpected turn of events

Woo! What was that? White's smarmy smile disappears with this unexpected turn of events. White didn't see that coming! He not only lost a bishop but his king and rook are both under attack, caught in a fork. Worse, he is in check and quicksand is swallowing him up. His mating attack cannot be delivered; he must get out of check first. White has only two moves to choose from, e2 or f1.

The f2-g1 black diagonal squares are under attack by Black's bishop and the d-file is attacked by Black's queen, so those squares are off limits.

Suddenly this one-sided game is upside down.

18. Ke2. White chooses to move his king to the e2 square, but f1 would be the same end result. Black's bishop on b7 is going to deliver the final blow.

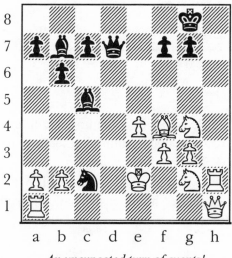

An unexpected turn of events!

18...Ba6 mate! Nowhere to run, nowhere to hide, every escape square under attack. Game over.

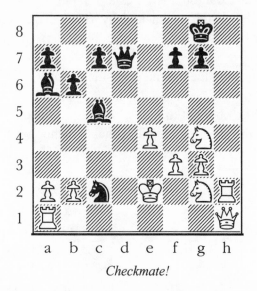

Checkmate!

White's mistake? He became so enamored with his next move, a checkmate in waiting, that he didn't bother to consider Black's threatening play. The penalty was not just the loss of a bishop, but the game itself! If White had played well, with his significant two-piece edge, he should easily have cruised to victory. But it was not to be.

8. THE OPENING: GOOD & BAD MOVES

To set yourself up for victory in a chess game, you need to get your pieces positioned properly in the opening. Bad moves will leave you in a weak position—vulnerable to attacks, loss of material, and serious threats to your king. Good moves will set you up for other good moves and put you in a position to launch a strong attack while maintaining a stout defense against your opponent.

It's like constructing a quality house. If you build the foundation strong, it can weather a storm; if you build it weak, it is vulnerable to collapse. This is true in chess as well. An opening with poorly placed pieces allows opponents to hammer away at your weak foundation, leaving the entire structure susceptible to implosion.

Your goal is to checkmate your opponent's king, however, it is rarely possible to achieve this in the opening. So instead, you must concentrate your efforts on maneuvering your pieces into the best possible positions for later success. Even in games where your opponent plays so poorly in the opening that you have an opportunity to deliver an early checkmate, that quick success still relies on proper development and positioning of your pieces.

With good development, good things can happen; with poor development, it is just the opposite—your chances of checkmating your opponent are lessened and his chances of checkmating you are enhanced. Whether a checkmate comes in the opening, the middle game, or later on in the endgame, a strong opening has a big say toward determining future victory.

In this chapter, I'll show you how to make good opening moves that will set you up for a strong game, and conversely, how to avoid damaging ones that can get exploited by your opponents. I'll also teach you the four-move mate, and even a two-move mate!

But first, let's get a good look at the best and worst moves for each piece at your disposal, starting with the pawns.

PAWN MOVES
1. Good Pawn Moves

The best pawn moves control and attack the center. As a beginner, your optimal opening move is to advance the pawn in front of the king or queen two spaces (1.e4 or 1.d4).*

These opening pawn moves achieve two important goals:

1. They attack the center.
2. They free up lines for other pieces to get into play.

You're looking to make the very best moves to start the game, and have two excellent choices. But which opening move is superior, the advance of the king pawn or the queen pawn?

The answer is neither!

* Black has a strong alternative to 1… e5 when White plays 1.e4 (the standard king-pawn opening and Black king-pawn response), and this move is 1...c5 (followed by 2...Nc6), the Sicilian Defense. While this stout defense is quite popular, to keep things simple for you as a beginner, we'll touch only on the 1…e5 opening as a counter to White's 1.e4. Later, as you further your studies, you might want to learn more about the Sicilian Defense and other sound White and Black opening moves.

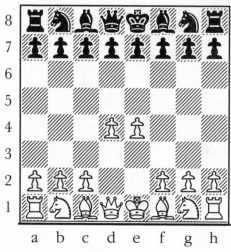

Either opening pawn move is good

They're both excellent moves and the choice of either one is simply a matter of preference. King pawn openings tend to lead toward freewheeling games with open lines and aggressive play. Queen pawn openings tend toward closed games, where small advantages and subtle maneuvers are worked behind the lines.

As you get more experienced with chess, you'll develop opening preferences for the style of play you prefer, or perhaps game plan a type of opening to use against a particular player. Ironically, many players sit down at a game with a preference for advancing the king's pawn and by whim move the queen's pawn instead! This regularly occurs not only with beginning players but with the world's very best players. Why the brain works this way? Adventure? Variety? Whim? Who knows!

Whatever pawn move White chooses, Black can safely answer with the corresponding pawn move, advancing his king pawn two spaces (1...e5) in response to White's king pawn opening (1.e4), or his queen pawn two spaces (1...d5) in response to White's queen pawn opening (1.d4). For example:

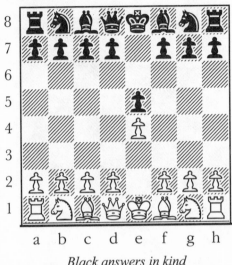

Black answers in kind

Moving the White pawn up two spaces in front of the king is the most common opening move, called as a group, **king pawn openings**, while the next most popular openings are led by the White pawn advancing two spaces in front of the queen, called—you guessed it—**queen pawn openings**.

What happens if White makes an opening move other than 1.e4 or 1.d4? No problem! Black should still advance his king or queen pawn two spaces (1…e5 or 1…d5), depending, of course, on which move is better for the situation.

2. Bad Pawn Moves

We know the good pawn opening moves, advancing two spaces up in front of the king or queen, and Black answering in kind.

The bad pawn moves? Just about every other pawn move.

You'll commonly see beginners move their rook pawns up two squares. For whatever reason, novices love these terrible opening forays. These rook pawn moves not only don't do anything worthwhile, but on top of that, they're worse than a wasted move—they weaken your position.

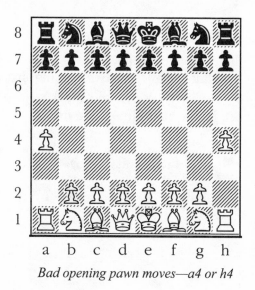

Bad opening pawn moves—a4 or h4

Here are two more bad pawn moves...

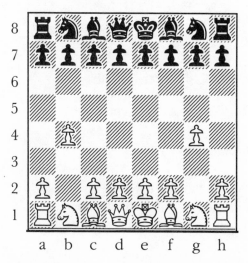

More bad opening pawn moves—b4 and g4

There are other terrible opening pawn moves, ones that don't further your strategic goals, or which weaken your position, but you get the idea.

What's worse than the above pawn moves?

Watch White's meltdown in this next opening disaster. After two epically bad moves by White, and Black's standard 1...e5 reply sandwiched in, the board looks like this:

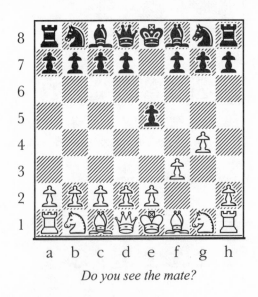

Do you see the mate?

Black has a finishing move. Do you see it?

2...Qh4!! Checkmate!

That's crazy. White moved just *twice* in the world's worst set of moves possible and he is already checkmated. Pawn up, queen out; good morning, good evening, good night.

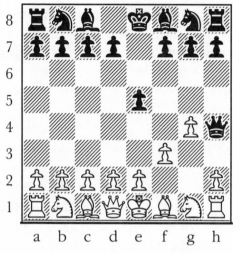

Checkmate in just two moves!

You'll rarely, if ever, see White make these two opening moves, but even so, these moves are instructive: They didn't achieve any of White's opening goals—development, attacking the center, or preparing to castle—nor did they accomplish anything other than set up the quickest and dumbest mate possible at the chessboard. Chess has an appropriate name for this quick ending: *Fool's Mate*.

CHAPTER NOTE

While I will typically concentrate on moves from White's perspective throughout this chapter, note that the same principles apply to Black's opening moves.

KNIGHT MOVES

Early in the game, knights are the most influential of the back row pieces—when used properly. They get into action faster than any other non-pawn piece and are almost always right in the middle of the action. Knights put pressure on and attack the center, vital warriors in pretty much every style of opening.

1. Good Knight Moves

In the beginning, the knights have several forward choices; toward the center, Nc3 or Nf3 for White, and Nc6 and Nf6 for Black, or along the edge, Na3 or Nh3 for White and Na6 or Nh6 for Black. It is the former set of moves, the ones that attack the center, that are the good moves. You could open with one of these moves, or both, as below.

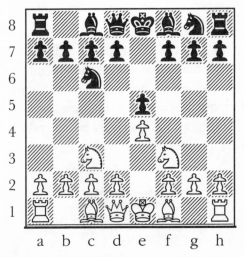

Good opening knight moves—f3 and/or c3

After each side opened with their pawn moving two squares in front of their king, White played **2.Nf3**. This move attacks Black's e-pawn. Black's standard reply, **2...Nc6** defends that pawn. White's next move, **3.Nc3**, defends White's own e-pawn and also attacks the central squares.

The good: the knights develop. More good: the knights attack the center. The bad: none.

2. Bad Knight Moves

There are good knight moves, and there are bad knight moves. It is so easy to make the good moves, why consider the bad? However, many beginners can't seem to help themselves and play the inferior version. Consider these offerings by White:

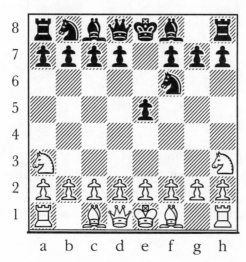

Bad opening knight moves—a3 and/or h3

No—don't do it! Don't make either knight move and certainly not both!

On the good side, the knights are developed, but on the bad side, they're *poorly* developed and don't attack the center. This game is only two moves in and already headed in a bad direction for White. If White decided to move his king pawn up two squares now, Black's f6 knight could snatch it right off. Free lunch.

There are even worse knight moves and for White, they look like this:

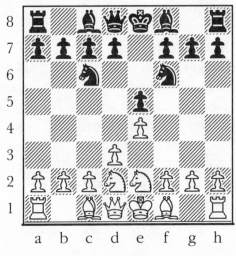

Awkward knight moves

These awkward knight moves, whether it is just one knight that occupies a square in front of the king or queen after the opening pawn move, or both of them in tandem, manage to be even worse than the first set of bad knight moves illustrated.

Why?

Well, for one thing, this type of awkward knight placement blocks the advancement of the bishops *and* the queen. For another, it will cost you an additional knight move to release any of those pieces.

These are bad spots for the knights this early in the game, worse choices than the "good knight moves" discussed earlier. There is no reason to consider them.

BISHOP MOVES

The bishop, like the knight, gets a lot of play in the opening. It is a strong offensive weapon, perfect for exerting pressure on your opponent. You'll see good bishop moves from players with sound ideas, and bad bishop moves from players with unsound ones. Let's look at both.

1. Good Bishop Moves

Good bishop moves attack the center or put pressure on opponent's pieces defending the center. Additionally, these attacking pieces, when pointed toward the king's area—the f7 square for White and the f2 square for Black, and later in the game, after castling, the h7 and h2 squares, respectively—pose a potential mating threat when aligned with other pieces. We'll see examples of this later on as we discuss other concepts.

Following are examples of two strong bishop moves:

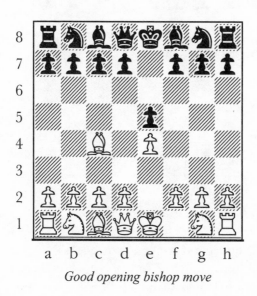

Good opening bishop move

White develops his bishop and puts it on a good square in the center of the board—classic and strong opening bishop play.

White has another strong opening bishop move, one that can be used to good advantage against the standard opening pawn and knight moves you'll typically see Black make.

After White's opening two moves, king pawn up two squares and knight out to the f3 square—and Black's classic reply 1... e5, 2...Nc6—White moves his white bishop to b5, attacking the Black knight defending the e5 pawn.

It looks like this:

1. e4   e5
2. Nf3   Nc6
3, Bb5

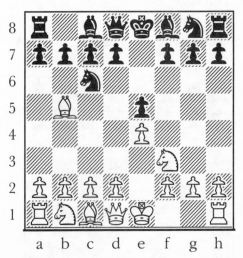

Bishop to b5, attacking Black's c6 knight

Black has several good moves here but a common one is to push the rook pawn up one square to chase away the bishop. The White bishop is pesky and Black wants it gone.

3   a6

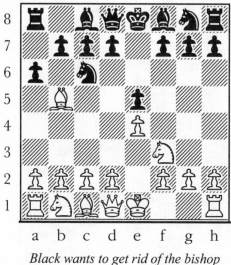

Black wants to get rid of the bishop

4.Bxc6   bxc6

But rather than run, which would be a weak move (why move there if only to retreat?), White captures the knight. Black takes White's bishop with his b-pawn, evening the exchange.

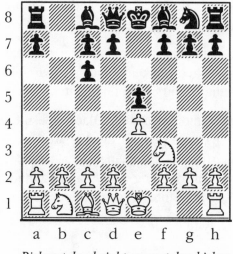

Bishop takes knight, pawn takes bishop

5. Nxe5. White picks up a snack, the free pawn at e5, which is no longer protected by Black's knight.

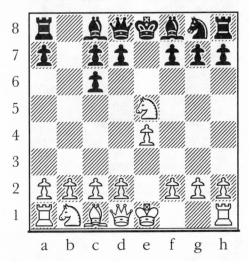

White's knight takes the unprotected e5 pawn

White has achieved some good things with this opening sequence:

- White is a pawn ahead after exchanging his bishop for Black's knight (the bishop and knight are about equal value).

- White has doubled up Black's pawns (the pawns on c6 and c7), which weakens Black's pawn link, a vulnerability that could be exploited later in the game.

- Five moves into the game, Black doesn't have a single piece developed nor even a pawn in the center—though that could change in a heartbeat with Black's next move being 6...d5 (among other possibilities)—while White has some minor development.

- White is ready to castle.

This is a nice opening sequence sure to annoy opponents. Black is by no means out of the game—there is a lot of chess still to be played and Black has plenty of counterplay—though White has a nice psychological edge with his small one pawn advantage.

2. Bad Bishop Moves

In the opening, beginners can find creative ways to make bad moves. Here, we'll look at two of them, one more dubious than the next.

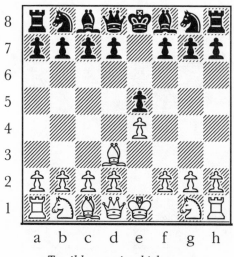

Terrible opening bishop move

a. 2.Bd3 (after 1.e4 and whatever move Black makes). This move can come later, on the third or fourth move, but the same principles below apply if the bishop occupies the d3 square before the queen pawn advances.

What the heck is this? Yes the bishop is out of the cocoon, but at the same time it blocks the forward movement of the queen's pawn, which in turn blocks not only the queen's pawn from advancing, but the pieces behind it! A terrible move. To develop the middle, you'll need to move the bishop an additional time, which costs you a move and momentum.

This game is only two moves old and already White is in a bad way. If you want to protect your central e4-pawn, there are superior moves, for example, moving the b1 knight to c3.

b. 3.Bb5 Hold on! Wasn't that just highlighted as a good move under "Good Bishop Moves"? Yes, that is correct, however, it's White's *next* move that determines whether the prior bishop move to b5 was a good or not quite so good move.

Let's revisit this move sequence.

1.e4 e5; 2.Nf3 Nc6; 3.Bb5 a6.

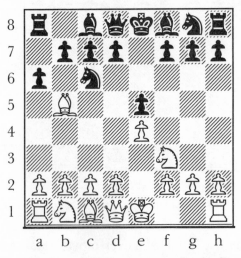

Opening bishop move: good or bad?

You come out with your bishop and Black tries to chase you away with his pawn. This is the same position we had arrived at earlier. It's what White does next that determines the soundness of his prior 3.Bb5 move.

Last time, White captured Black's knight with his bishop. This time White has a different idea, a less sound one.

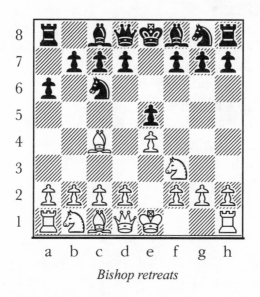

Bishop retreats

4. Bc4. White has chosen to retreat, in effect, wasting a move. Black's possible response of a6 should have been considered. If you're going to move your bishop to b4, do it the first time, and if you're going to move it to a5, the plan should be to attack the knight and grab the extra pawn (as discussed earlier in "Good Bishop Moves").

The takeaway here is that you need to think and plan ahead, not only considering your move possibilities and ideas, but how your opponent might respond to your moves. As you become more experienced as a chess player, your "vision" at the table will improve and make you a stronger player.

This "bad" opening move was not horrible in the sense of the other bad moves we covered—let's call it less than ideal—but the potential pinning square for your bishop at b5 is now protected and you let Black's a6 pawn get there as a free move.

Let's move on now to the rook.

ROOK MOVES

Rooks start out the game trapped in the corners, being of little use. But their time will come. Let's see what some good and bad rook moves look like.

1. Good Rook Moves

After you castle, you'll get your first rook in play, usually the kingside one, which will help attack the center files or other strategic open files as they may develop. Later, in the middle game, and definitely by the endgame, your second rook will develop and play a powerful role in shaping the direction of the chess battle.

In the diagram below, White's kingside rook, freed by castling, moved to e1 (from f1) to help defend the e-pawn and pressure the center.

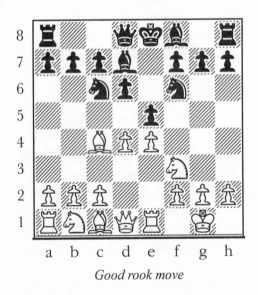

Good rook move

2.Bad Rook Moves

In the game below, White, with no strategic insights and an unhealthy amount of impatience, worked around the rook's initial limitation by combining a whole bunch of bad moves together. Forgetting Black's moves for a bit, watch this horror show unfold. White's first three moves—**h4, Rh3, Rg3**—create this unsightly mess:

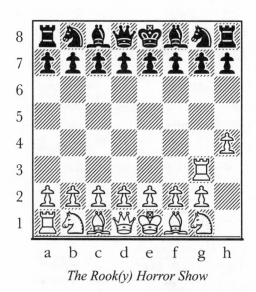

The Rook(y) Horror Show

In addition to the rook being situated in an exposed and funky position, this sequence is a complete disaster. Consider:

- Nothing about White's game is developed.

- About the worst pawn move possible has been made.

- The center is not being attacked.

- Multiple moves have been wasted.

- The g3 rook is in an awkward place.

That's a lot of strategic violations by White for this early in the game. With the way this game is developing, if you're Black in this match, you better win this game.

QUEEN MOVES

The queen is your most powerful piece and you must guard its safety with your chess life. A queen for queen exchange is fine, but exchanging a queen for any other piece invites an almost sure defeat. In the opening, given the importance of the queen, you want to keep its movement quiet, coming out only to grab a piece or move toward a powerful attack or mate.

1. Good Queen Moves

In the game below, Black captures White's knight in the center and there is only one piece that can even the exchange—the queen. In this case, go get it. That's what the queen is there for, after all. Here's the move order:

1.e4 e5; 2.Nf3 Nc6; 3.d4. On the third move White gets aggressive and runs the queen pawn out two squares.

Setting up

3...exd4; 4.Nxd4 Nxd4. Black's pawn takes the offering, White's knight captures back, and Black's knight takes White's knight.

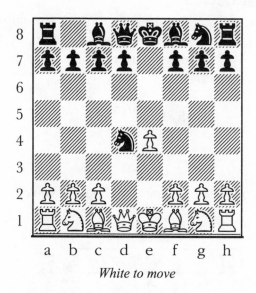

White to move

Black is a knight ahead but there is no reason to leave it like that.

5.Qxd4. It is White's turn and he uses the queen to capture White's knight and even the score. This is a good use of the queen.

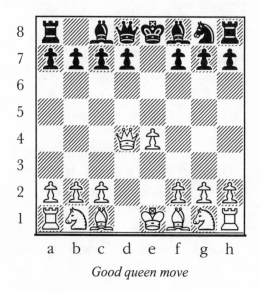

Good queen move

2. Bad Queen Moves

A common beginner's mistake is to bring out the queen too early. It is your most powerful piece so you're thinking, why not? The problem is that you violate multiple strategic concepts. Consider the following:

1.e4	**e5**
2.Nc3	**Nc6**
3.Qg4?	

White's queen to the g4 square is a bad move. You'll soon see why.

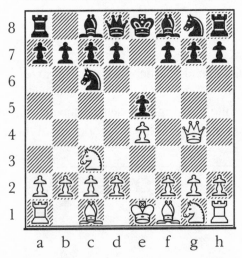

White brings the queen out too early

3...d6. Black advances his queen pawn, opening up the c8 bishop for a direct attack on White's queen. If White doesn't see this discovered attack, for example, he moves his bishop out or advances his d-pawn, Black will take off White's queen. A player bringing out his queen this early will often be caught in these kinds of blunders and the game will essentially be over just three moves in!

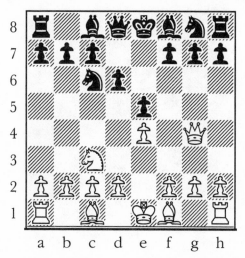

Queen attacked by bishop through discovered pawn move

4.Qh5   **Nf6**

White's queen moves to h5

Really?

White sees the discovered attack, a small miracle perhaps, but doesn't learn his lesson. Black answers by developing another piece, his knight at f6, and launching another attack against the beleaguered queen.

At the same time, Black's f6 knight, doing double duty, attacks White's e4 pawn as well.

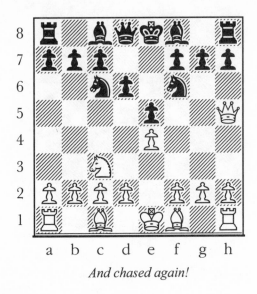

And chased again!

5. Qe2. White's queen is running out of safe squares and retreats to e2.

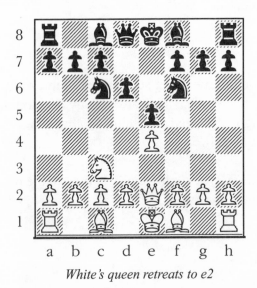

White's queen retreats to e2

Forgetting for a second that this queen retreat is another horrible move, since it blocks the development of White's f1 bishop, look at what White has done.

Three wasted moves while Black developed nicely—and it is Black's turn!

One of the most damaging moves in the opening is bringing a queen out too early and you just saw how bad this turned out. There are even worse results, courtesy of a bad blunder or an opponent's clever trap, that could lead to the loss of a queen! And that often will be the case.

There are many variations of a queen coming out too early and getting chased around the board while an opponent develops, and most of them end badly for the side that had prematurely advanced the queen.

Learn this lesson well: The queen should only come out of its hole when it is necessary, either to capture a piece, defend against or avoid some tricky situation, or later, once the battle marches into the middle game, to put pressure on the opposition as part of a coordinated attack with other pieces.

And now on to the last piece on the board, the one and only king.

KING MOVES

Except for castling, which you want to go about fairly quickly (in the first four to ten moves), you generally want to avoid moving the king in the early going of a game. If you're in check and have no other choice but to move the king, or your king can capture a piece that no other piece can grab, then yes, get your king in motion.

Let's look at a few situations:

1. Good King Moves

a. Castling

We have talked about this plenty. That's almost always a great king move.

b. Avoiding Check

In the situation below, White has no choice but to get his king out of danger. Black's bishop has just moved from c5 to b4 and put White's king in check.

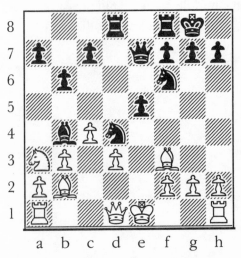

King has no choice but to move

There is no choice for White but to move the king out of check. Sure, the queen could block the check, but that's almost certain death—you can't lose your queen and get only a bishop in return!

This king capture is only a "good" king move inasmuch as there are no better options available. It's not an ideal situation for White but at least it was a forced move, not a voluntary election to negate his castling chances and move his king to an undesirable square. By the way, White's only move is to f1 (e2 is under attack by Black's d4 knight).

c. Capturing Material

When the king has an opportunity to grab material, it's usually an excellent move, or at least, the best move in a given situation. Consider these opening moves:

1.e4	**e5**
2.d4	**Nc6**
3.Bc4	**Be2**
4.Bxf7+	

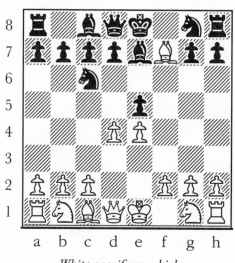

White sacrifices a bishop

White has just sacrificed a bishop on the fourth move, disrupting Black's safe haven. The king can either take the bishop or move to f8. Of course Black takes—that bishop is too sweet a treat to pass up! There will be no castling for Black, not that Black has a choice at this juncture, but for a bishop advantage, Black doesn't mind the inconvenience. It is up to White to make something of this sacrifice and Black must be very careful here as there are serious traps waiting if the wrong moves are made.

If Black can avoid some pitfalls in the next few moves and exchange a bunch of pieces for equal material as the game moves on, Black is in good position for a win. This was not a good White sacrifice, but hey, Black will take the free piece!

THE 4-MOVE MATE

I promised you the four-move mate and here it is. Actually, it has a name, *Scholar's Mate*. The queen is a vital piece in the mate and it combines with a bishop to finish off the opponent's king.

The four-move checkmate is often seen among rank beginners who don't recognize the lethal combination developing right in front of them. At higher levels of play, you won't see players bringing out the queen this early without a compelling reason, but among novices, a wandering queen in the early going is a common occurrence.

White opens with two basic developing moves, advancing the king pawn and bringing a bishop out into an attacking position. Black responds with good moves as well, but it is White's third move, the queen to h5, that spells trouble for an unprepared opponent.

1.e4   e5
2.Bc4   Nc6
3.Qh5

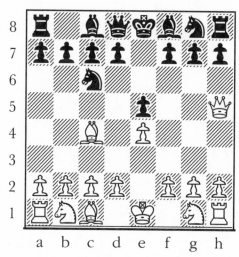

White will mate if Black makes the wrong move

Against a good player, bringing out the queen this early is a terrible move. It sets the queen up to get chased around while Black develops, or worse, to get captured as the result of a blunder. Earlier, we saw a queen being relentlessly chased to the detriment of White's game. Here, however, Black is inexperienced and falls into the trap.

3...a6. Forget that Black's move doesn't accomplish anything. (A common move for Black might instead be 1...Nf6, attacking White's queen, but regardless, that move would also be a disaster in this situation and won't deter White's next play.) Actually, forget everything—game over.

4. Qxf7 checkmate! The queen takes the pawn at f7 and that's all she wrote. This is the classic queen-and-bishop four-move checkmate.

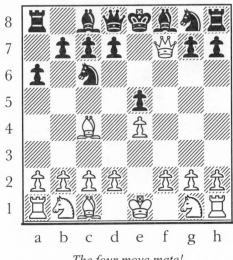

The four move mate!

Black had various moves that could have prevented this mate, but ignoring the threat was not one of them.

CHESS OPENINGS

There are hundreds, even thousands of named chess openings, and it would be good for your progress to start familiarizing yourself with some standard ones as both a Black player and a White player. I've covered a few here without naming them or going into too much detail, but for your next foray into deepening your chess knowledge, a good book on chess openings would certainly help you along your path as a chess player. On our website, www.cardozabooks.com, you will find many good ones that we publish.

If you become super serious about chess, you could spend years and years getting a deeper understanding of chess openings. In fact, the greatest players in the world devote countless thousands of hours familiarizing themselves with their many nuances.

But as a beginner, you only need to know the principles of good opening play to have a good start to a chess game. I think we took a big step in that direction. Let's now move on to the middle game and look at some ideas and options to increase your skills and help you become a stronger player.

9. MIDDLE GAME: STRATEGY & TACTICS

The middle game is an indeterminate period in a chess game where you have emerged out of the opening position—by now you should have developed your pieces, castled, and hopefully, established a reasonably strong position from which to move forward toward your quest for victory.

If you're against a player who has violated the basic principles of chess, you'll already have an advantage in the game. And if you're against a player who has learned chess the correct way, and played strongly as you have played—making strategically correct moves in the opening—you have a good battle on your hands!

Okay, you're out of the opening, the game is in front of you and you're saying to yourself:

Now what?

Of course, you're always looking to end the game with a brilliant mating attack, but meanwhile, in the middle game, as you maneuver your pieces into strong attacking positions, you're looking for opportunities to capture your opponent's pieces and gain a material edge. In this chapter, we'll see how to do just that.

Let's get to it!

MIDDLE GAME OBJECTIVES

One of your strategic goals as you work toward the ultimate goal of capturing your opponent's king is to remove more of your opponent's pieces than he does of yours. When you're ahead in material by a knight or bishop, or in the endgame by even as little as a pawn, you have enough to win the game if you play well. That doesn't mean you will win, because an opponent may checkmate you with clever play, but if you're careful and play a strong game, you *should* win.

The main focus of your chess battle, summed up below, is two-fold:

1. **You try to checkmate your opponent:** You're always looking for ways to end the game decisively with a checkmate, but those situations are not always there for the taking. So on the way to this goal...
2. **You try to gain material superiority.** If you capture more pieces from your opponent than he captures from you, you'll have an advantage big enough to force a win later in the game.

FORKS, PINS, & OTHER TRICKY PLAYS

At the beginning levels, many pieces are lost through blunders. For example, a player leaves a piece *hanging*, that is, unprotected, and you swoop in and remove it from the board. But low hanging fruit is not always going to be there for the picking. Sometimes you have to go get those pieces through your own clever moves.

Setting traps, like forks and pins, is the bread and butter for chess players trying to gain a material advantage over their opponents. Let's look at some of the great traps you can use to gain the upper hand.

THE MIGHTY FORKS

A *fork* is a tactic in which one piece simultaneously attacks two more valuable pieces. Here are three good forks to add to your arsenal.

1. Knight Fork in Action

The knight fork is a beautiful thing. When you can grab a free rook, or even better, a queen, your opponent is in trouble and the game is yours for the taking!

Can you find the knight fork here? Black to move.

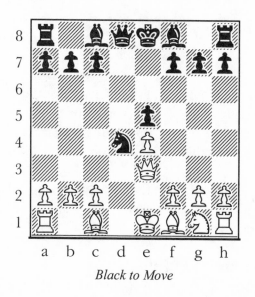

Black to Move

...Nxc2+. Bam! Not just a double fork, but a triple fork—king, rook, *and* queen!

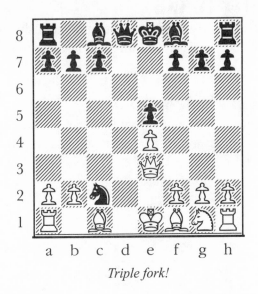

Triple fork!

White's king must move and the queen must die! If you play solid chess from here, your overwhelming edge should lead to victory. After White's king moves to e2, Black's knight takes the queen at e3. If White plays on more carnage will follow.

If White makes the unfortunate choice of moving his king to d1, Black's knight takes the queen and has an additional fork on the king and f1 bishop!

2. Bishop Fork in Action

The knight is not the only piece that can get in on the action. Here's a nifty bishop fork that presents itself to White. White to move.

Do you see the fork?

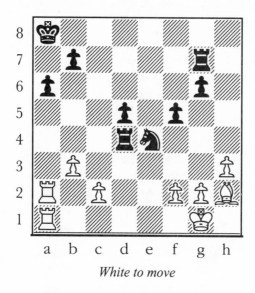

White to move

White's bishop from h2 to e5.

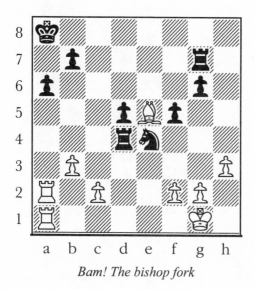

Bam! The bishop fork

Before White's move, material was even. However, no matter what move Black makes, he is going to lose a rook outright.

Even if Black could capture the bishop after White took off one of his rooks—which he can't in this position—the uneven exchange would still be a good get for White since rooks are more valuable than bishops.

3. Pawn Fork in Action

Hey, don't forget about the pawns! They can get in on the fork action as well. In the game below, a pawn is poised to make some trouble.

Do you White's nifty pawn move?

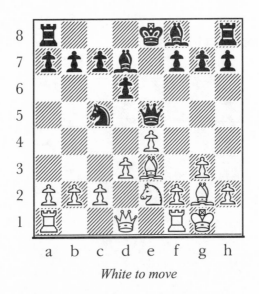

White to move

White's pawn to **d4**.

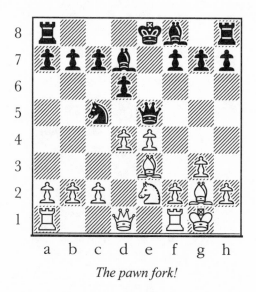

The pawn fork!

And the fork! The pawn fork is beautiful. White nets himself a piece for a pawn. Obviously Black will move the queen out of trouble and when he does, it's time for the tasty knight snack.

THE DASTARDLY PINS

A *pin* is a trap in which one piece is under attack but cannot move without exposing a more valuable piece to capture. Pins are powerful plays, especially when they lead to a big material gain or even checkmate.

1. A Bishop Pin

The classic opening pin is a bishop advancing to the fifth rank (b5 or g5) as White (or fourth rank, b4 or g4, as Black), pinning a knight. The pinned knight cannot move because it would expose the king or queen, whichever is pinned, to check or capture. Defenders can block the pin by moving a bishop behind the knight, defuse it by pushing up a rook pawn one square to chase the bishop, or force the pinning piece to exchange.

If left unattended, a pin paralyzes the knight, rendering it unable to move. Here is a small consequence of a knight being pinned by the bishop.

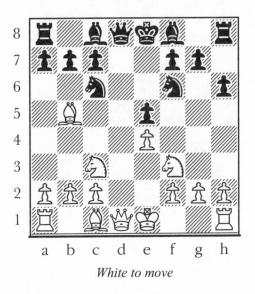

White to move

5.Nxe5. White takes advantage of the pin by capturing the e5 pawn with his knight.

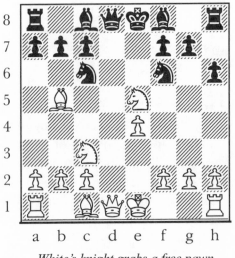

White's knight grabs a free pawn

Normally, Black's defending c6 knight would capture White's knight for a profitable exchange. However, Black's knight is pinned—moving it would expose the king to check, which is not allowed—and thus, he is unable to defend e5. White gets a free center pawn.

White now has two pieces attacking Black's c6 knight. If Black doesn't pay attention to this threat, watch what happens. Black is eager to castle, which is almost always a good idea, but here it is premature. He has more pressing needs.

5...Bb4. Black moves his bishop to b4, creating his own pin on White's c3 knight. This would free the king to castle on the next move and remove White's pin. However, it's not the best move at this time and Black will soon find out why.

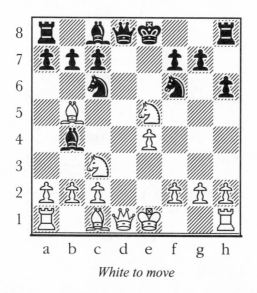

White to move

6.Nxc6. White's e5 knight takes Black's c6 knight. **6...bxc6.** Black recaptures with his b7 pawn. If Black ignored White's troublesome c6 knight, not only will he lose the knight, but Black's queen will be lost on the next play (the knight can capture the queen if it is not moved). So Black makes the obvious capture.

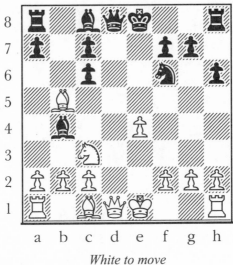

White to move

7.Bxc6+. White's bishop takes the c6 pawn—a king and rook fork! Black is in check and blocks the attack by moving his bishop to d7. White's bishop takes the a8 rook and Black's queen captures the bishop at a8. Black has just won that exchange. If Black, instead, made the terrible decision of moving his king, White grabs the rook for free (since the Black queen is being blocked by its own bishop from defending the rook). Plus Black can no longer castle and has a messed up position.

Black would have been spared this entire headache by simply moving his bishop to b2 to protect against this pin in the first place. Instead, White has surged ahead with a nice advantage.

2. Another Bishop Pin

This next situation creates a more serious problem. White's rook is under attack by Black's queen along the long black diagonal, but the rook is safe since it is defended by White's d3 knight.

Or is it?

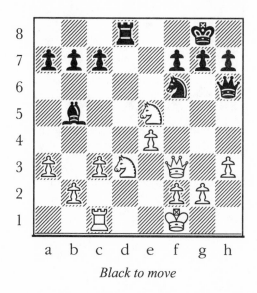

Black to move

As it turns out, the answer is no, the rook is definitely not safe. White ignored the pin set up on the turn before when Black moved his bishop **...Bb5**. White, a pawn-snatcher at heart and eager to grab material, had ignored the pin when he answered with **Nxe5**, snatching Black's e5 pawn with his knight.

A mistake!

...Qxc1+. Black's queen sweeps across the long black diagonal and takes the c1 rook! White reaches for the knight to recapture and then realizes, too late, that that move won't work!

White's knight on d3 cannot capture the offending queen—it is pinned by the Black bishop at b5! White's rook is lost, a casualty of his knight being pinned.

White's king is in check and his only play is to move the king to e2.

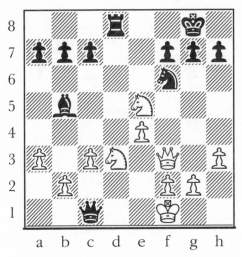

White just lost a rook and is in check

Black is now up a rook, a significant advantage, and White's king is on the run.

3. Rook Pin

White is ahead by two pieces in this game with a massive attack waiting to be unleashed, but he's actually the one in trouble!

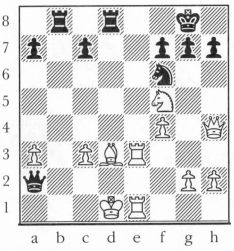

Black to move. He has a surprise.

White is not concerned about Black's queen coming down to the first rank. He can simply move his king to e2 (with his un-blocked rook at e1 now attacking the White queen) and after, skip the king to the safety of f1. With two pieces to the advantage and his pieces lined up nicely, White sees a clear victory ahead.

The problem: *It is Black's turn* and Black has a clever move waiting in the dance line. It is not however, the queen check White had anticipated and was eager to defend.

Do you see the crushing blow?

36...Rb1! Checkmate!

White is stunned as Black exclaims, "Checkmate!" and sends his b8 rook down to the first rank on b1. White's first instinct is to remove the offending rook with his well-placed bishop on d3, but then realizes his bishop is pinned by Black's d8 rook—and his goose is cooked.

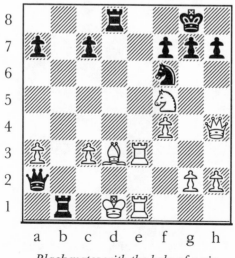

Black mates with the help of a pin

THE DEADLY DISCOVERED CHECK

A *discovered check* occurs when you put an opponent's king in check simply by moving one of your own pieces out of the way, the *blocking piece*, and opening a clear line of attack by the piece secreted behind it. The beauty of the discovered check is that the blocking piece has no fear of capture because your opponent must defend against the discovered check, leaving the mischievous blocking piece free reign over the board, its next move harboring devastating consequences.

Let's see what this looks like...

1. Discovered Check by Rook

In the diagram below, Black's king would be in check by White's rook if not for the White knight, which is blocking the action. It is White's turn to move and Black is in big trouble.

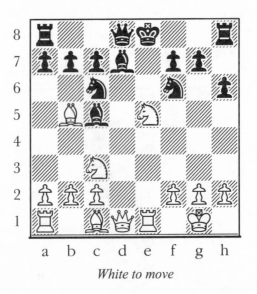

White to move

When White moves his knight at e5, Black will be in check from White's e1 rook. He must either move his king or block the check. Black's choice of moves makes no difference to White because the destruction on its way cannot be stopped. White's blocking knight is free to go to any square it chooses without fear of repercussion while Black figures out how to stop the check. The knight move will prove to be the end of any realistic chance Black has to win this game.

Watch the tsunami roll in.

Nxc6!

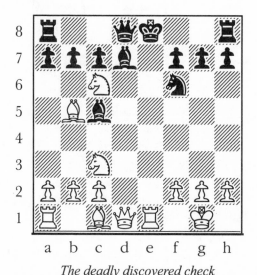

The deadly discovered check

One piece down! White's e5 knight takes Black's c6 knight. Black must defend against the discovered check by White's e1 rook—there is no choice in the matter. Regardless of the move Black chooses, White's attacking knight will take off Black's queen at d8, or if the Black queen chooses to block the check at e2, then at e2. Then it will be two pieces down! Black has lost control of this game and the devastation isn't even finished yet.

A disaster for Black, but he ran out of options once he allowed the discovered check alignment by his wily opponent.

2. Uncovering a Discovered Queen Attack

Back when we showed castling, we ended up with the following position after White's sixth move.

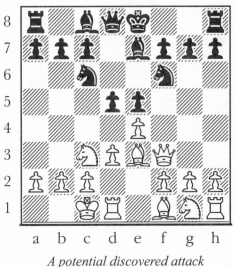

A potential discovered attack

Black must be very careful here. Look at the hidden danger of White's rook lined up with Black's queen on the d-file. A direct line between the two is not imminent, but things can change in a hurry. White is hoping Black will free things up by taking his e4 pawn, the beginning of a pawn exchange. And indeed he does.

6...dxe4. Black can no longer resist the pawn capture and he takes White's e4 pawn. **7.dxe4.** White captures back with his d-pawn. But danger lurks! The pawn capture exposes Black's queen to attack by White's rook at d1. The pawn exchange is perfectly fine for Black, but if he doesn't see the discovered attack on his queen, he'll be dealt a devastating blow. (Note also the pawn fork Black missed by passing on the pawn exchange and instead pushing the pawn up to d4, forking White's bishop and knight! Black could also move his bishop to g4, attacking White's queen and capturing the rook behind it when it moves.)

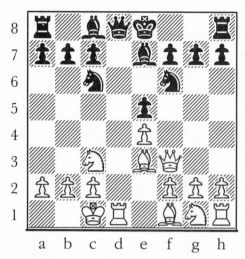

Black must not sleep on this discovered attack

STRATEGIES WHEN YOU'RE AHEAD IN MATERIAL

When you have a piece or more advantage, trading material is a solid roadmap to victory. If a bishop can be captured and it will cost you a bishop or a knight, make the exchange. Similarly, trade a knight for a bishop or knight, a rook for a rook and a queen for a queen. As the game winds down, your material advantage becomes relatively greater each time an additional piece gets eliminated from the game.

With just a few pieces left and you having more material than your opponent, the game becomes a mismatch—and yours for the taking.

Exchanges accomplish two things.

1. They simplify the board.
2. Your opponent has fewer weapons to use against you.

When you're in the middle of a terrific attack with an excellent possibility of delivering a crushing checkmate, you make an exception to the rule of exchanging when you're ahead, instead avoiding exchanges unless absolutely necessary. You want your entire army in play and focused on bringing home the final checkmate.

However, if no checkmate is imminent, then back to the rule— trade, trade, trade!

Let's say you're ahead by a rook. You then exchange a bishop, rook and knight for your opponent's bishop, rook and knight and then, with some clever play, force an equal exchange of queens and the remaining bishops. Assuming the pawns are even at four apiece, here is where you stand.

You (White): King, four pawns, knight, rook
Him (Black): King, four pawns, knight

You have a huge advantage here, one so great, that all advanced players facing this material disparity would immediately re-sign against similarly strong opponents unless they either had a great attack or an amazing position that would lead to mate. This game is lost and no strong player would waste his or his opponent's time pursuing such a fruitless battle.

However, at the lower levels, among beginners, anything can happen. When you're ahead, your job is to make sure that any-thing *doesn't* happen. Complicated positions, especially against clever opponents, leave room for brilliant plays and surprise stratagems. You lessen these possibilities by removing pieces and opportunities.

Let's say you then successfully exchange the knights and two pawns. The remaining material for you and your opponent is as follows:

You (White): King, two pawns, rook
Him (Black): King, two pawns

A rook advantage

Now your strategy is simple. Either of two ways will bring you a win:

1. Trade off the pawns and use your rook and king to checkmate your opponent. We'll see how to achieve this in the next chapter.

2. Use the leverage of your rook to promote one of your pawns to a queen. (Feel free to remove your opponent's pawns while you're at it so they can't promote.) A king is no match against a king and rook, and certainly no match against a king, queen *and* rook. With this overwhelming edge in material, you should make quick and easy work of your opponent.

STRATEGIES WHEN YOU'RE BEHIND IN MATERIAL

When you're behind in material, you do exactly the opposite of when you're ahead—you attempt to preserve your pieces!

The more weapons you have, the better chance you have of winning. Or think of it this way: If you had an army of 1,000 soldiers against an equivalent army of 1,000 soldiers, the loss of one or two of your men, or even of ten men, would be close to negligible given the overall mass.

However, with just seven total non-pawn pieces for each player, the loss of one uncompensated piece—your six pieces against the opponent's seven—would be significant. If four pieces were then evenly exchanged, so now your opponent had three non-pawn pieces to your two—the mismatch would be far greater.

You prefer to play a *closed position* when behind in material, that is, a position where the pawns form strong barriers and movement is restricted. It lessens your opponent's material edge.

On the other hand, an *open position*, a board with wide open lines for pieces to maneuver, is to be avoided if possible. Open positions benefit players with superior firepower and make it easier to force trades.

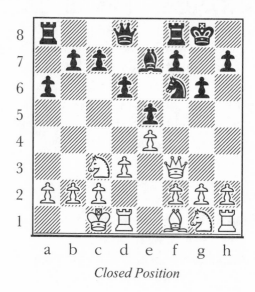

Closed Position

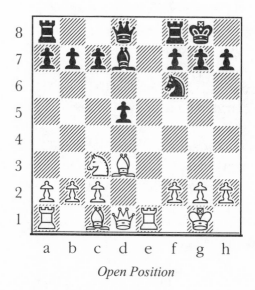

Open Position

In both diagrams, Black is down a piece, however, the board with the closed position gives Black better chances of preserving material and equalizing the game.

STRATEGIES AGAINST BETTER PLAYERS

A superior opponent has more skills and more tricks up his sleeve to outmaneuver you at the chessboard. You attempt to nullify some of that edge by keeping the position as simple as you can—minimizing his edge in complex positions—and by trading pieces of equal value at every opportunity. You'll look to trade knights for knights or bishops, bishops for knights or bishops, rooks for rooks, and queens for queens.

Trading pieces of equal value achieves two things:

1. **The board gets less complicated.** That's good for you. A less complicated board makes it's easier for you to analyze the position and harder for your opponent to make subtle maneuvers that you won't see until the damage is done. Complicated positions and more pieces favor better players. You try to keep it simple.

2. **Better players have fewer weapons at their disposal.** While you do too, fewer moving parts softens his edge.

If this strategy sounds identical to the approach you should take when you're ahead in material, well, it is!

Trading pieces of equal value will not equalize the battle between you and a superior player, but it gives you more of a fighting chance to have a competitive game. Rise to your best level and try to give your opponent the best game you have in you. And maybe, just maybe, you'll surprise him with a superlative performance and take home the point yourself!

This seems like a good time as any to talk about the biggest mismatch of my chess career, when I played against a vastly superior opponent in a complete mismatch.

10. AVERY VERSUS THE U.S. CHAMPION

In 1998, my company, Cardoza Publishing, as a top publisher of chess books for beginning and intermediate players, sponsored the U.S. Chess Championships in Hawaii. All the top U. S. players were at the championship including, at the time the top under-10 and under-14 players in the United States, a who's who of young budding talent, many who would go on to become notable players and grandmasters, such as superstar Hikaru Nakamura, 10-years-old at the time, who became a multi-time U.S. champion.

A match was arranged between myself and Joel Benjamin, the extant United States Chess Champion and the chess architect behind Big Blue, the computer program that eventually defeated World Champion Garry Kasparov. There were international masters and grandmasters crowded around the board—I remember two of my authors were there, Life Master Eric Schiller, who had arranged the match and the sponsorship, and Grandmaster Eduard Gufeld—not because the game would be interesting on its own merits, but to relax and unwind after some serious matches earlier in the day.

Note: I had no chance in hell of beating Joel Benjamin, the best player in the United States, and would have had no chance even if he had been stark, raving half-blind drunk—which he certainly wasn't. I'm not a bad player, but this is the champion of the United States we're talking about. This was a huge mismatch, but the exhibition was arranged so we could all have a little fun.

My goal was to keep it reasonably close for fifteen moves and, if I could do that, I could claim a moral victory.

Well, Joel Benjamin was not drunk, and the kibitzers, world-class players that gave me a helping hand on a few moves, were not enough supporting firepower for this gross mismatch. I didn't get to my fifteen-move goal. I'm not sure I made it to ten moves before the game become too one-sided to reasonably continue. Material was still equal, but Joel's position was overwhelming superior. I could see where this was going and there was no point in continuing. I resigned perhaps a dozen moves into the match.

There is no shame in losing to the U.S. Champion. In this instance, my opponent was so far over my skill level, it made no difference how well I played—or how poorly he played—the result was inevitable. My goal was to keep the game competitive for as long as I could. Everyone—myself, Joel and the world-class kibitzers—had fun, even though I didn't last quite as long as I would have liked.

The point of this story?

Chess is about having fun and taking on challenges, with those challenges sometimes being well over your skill level. If you get the opportunity to play a really good player, make the most of it, play your very best, and enjoy the experience for as long as you can stay competitive in the game!

11. HOW TO CHECKMATE YOUR OPPONENT

To win at chess, you must know how to checkmate your opponent's king. There are numerous ways to achieve this and they all involve recognition of potential mating patterns and, sometimes, a bit of chicanery to maneuver into those positions. The checkmating patterns we'll cover in this chapter will appear over and over again in your chess-playing life so familiarize yourself with them and get ready to put them into action!

1. BACK RANK MATE WITH ROOK OR QUEEN

Once you get into the middle game, with pieces developed and a battle raging on in the middle of the board, you'll often find a situation similar to the one shown below. See how White's rook is lined up to advance eight squares in a straight line?

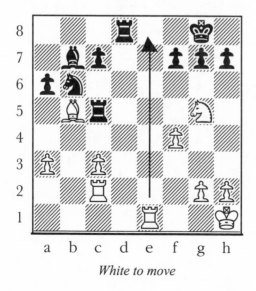

White to move

If somehow, White can get Black's rook off the 8th rank (at d8), the situation will be grave for Black. Black had just moved, pushing his a7 pawn to a6, and attacking White's b6 bishop. This gave us the position in the above diagram. Black waits on White to answer with his own move.

27. Bd3. White moves his bishop from b5 to d3, away from Black's threatening a6 pawn, while, in coordination with his knight at g5, threatening Black's h7 pawn.

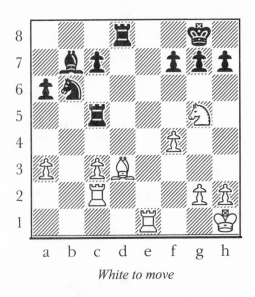

White to move

27...Rxd3. Black can't believe his good fortune! White has left his bishop hanging at d3, completely undefended. Black immediately spots this and swoops down to grab the bishop with his rook. It's been a hard fought game and White finally buckled under the pressure. Black is now up a piece.

Actually, however, White is the color with the good fortune — Black fell for the trap! When Black's rook abandoned the 8th rank, he opened it up to this move...

28. Re8 checkmate! White's rook flies down to e8, giving Black's king no place to hide and no way to protect itself. Black's king is completely trapped—checkmate!

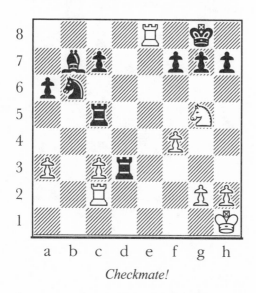

Checkmate!

The key checkmating situation you look for is as follows:

1. The king trapped behind three pawns on the back rank with no escape route—the typical position after castling.
2. No rook or queen protecting the rank on which the king sits.
3. Your own rook or queen ready to pounce in for the checkmate.

2. BACK RANK MATE: OVERWHELMING THE DEFENDER

You can deliver a back rank mate by luring an opponent's piece off an end rank, as White just did in the above game, or by overwhelming the defender for the same result. Let's take the same game with a different Black response and show you how to deliver a checkmate.

Here's the position:

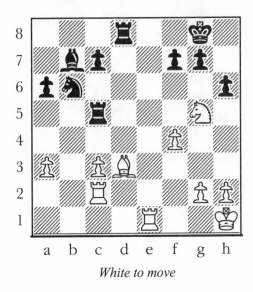

White to move

27...h6. This time, after White's bishop retreats to d3, Black sees the danger of capturing the bishop and doesn't take the bait. Instead, Black pushes his h7 rook pawn forward to chase away the bothersome knight camped near his king. The h7 square, now unoccupied, also serves as a potential escape square against a back rank mate on Black's king.

But White is still cooking in the kitchen.

28. Rce2. White moves his rook from c2 to e2, doubling up the rooks. **28...hxg5.** Black quickly grabs the knight, putting him up a piece, but it is a poisoned piece he'll soon choke on. Black is so focused on that g6 knight and so pleased with himself for not falling into White's trap, that he ignored the trouble brewing on the e-file.

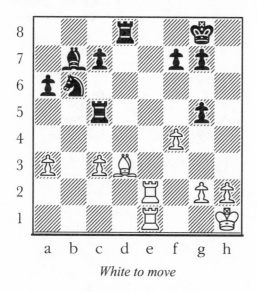

White to move

29. Re8+! White's rook advances all the way down, check!

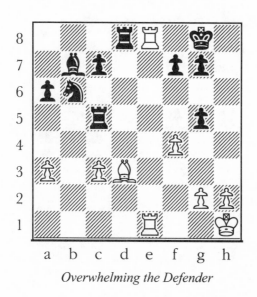

Overwhelming the Defender

29...Rxe8. Black has no choice but to take White's rook with his own rook.

30.Rxe8—checkmate! White's e1 rook takes back. (Black's h7 escape square is covered by White's d3 bishop—game over!)

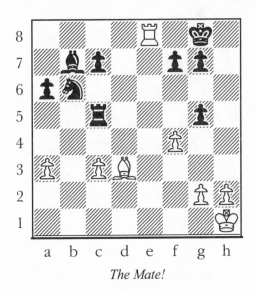

The Mate!

3. BISHOP-AND-QUEEN MATE

The queen and bishop work well together. You just line them up and BAM!—you pull off a mate. Consider the following:

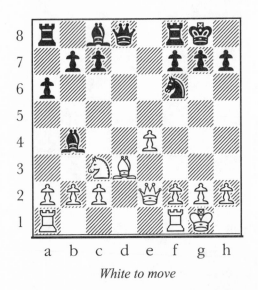

White to move

10. e5   **Nd7**
11. Qe4

White moves a pawn forward to attack Black's knight at f6. At least, that is what Black sees. Black retreats the knight to the d7 square rather than lose it. White counters by moving his queen to the space formerly occupied by the pawn, attacking Black's bishop at b4.

The position looks like this:

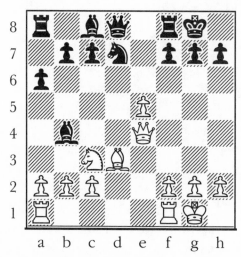

White's queen attacks the bishop!

11...Ba5. Black sees the queen's attack on his bishop and backs the bishop up to a5. But what Black doesn't see is that White secretly lined up the bishop and queen in a mating formation.

And now the *coup de grace.*

12. Qxh7 checkmate!

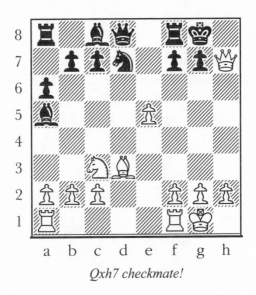

Qxh7 checkmate!

You see what happened? White got Black's knight on f6 to move—it was defending the key h7 square—then lined up his queen and bishop under the ruse of attacking other pieces, and came down for a powerful finish.

4. ENDGAME MATE WITH TWO ROOKS

With two rooks working together in a two-rook-advantage endgame, your opponent has little chance of surviving if you know how to complete the mate. Rooks on open ranks or files create barriers that cannot be crossed.

Watch how Black closes in on the White king and ends his misery.

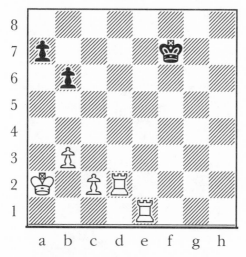

Endgame mate using two rooks

33. Rf2+ Kg6; 34.Rg1+ Kh5. Black moves his rook from d2 to f2, checking the king. Black's king moves closer to the edge and then closer again when the e1-square rook moves to the g1 square, checking the king and cutting off another file.

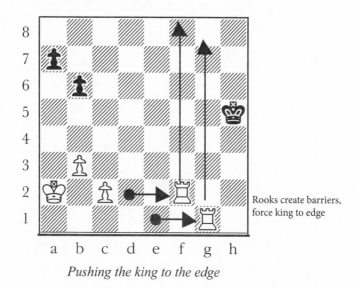

Rooks create barriers, force king to edge

Pushing the king to the edge

White's rooks, working in tandem, cut off the king's breathing room and march him to the abyss.

There is just one more move needed. Do you see it?

35. Rh2 mate! The rook on the f-file delivers the killing blow, the final asphyxiation complete. Precise, forced, and quick—there was nothing Black could do.

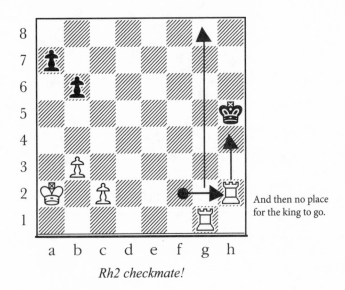

And then no place for the king to go.

Rh2 checkmate!

5. ENDGAME ROOK-AND-KING MATE

With just a rook and a king against a king, your two pieces must
work together. Your strategy is to push the opposing king into
a corner so the final blow can be delivered. Your rook restricts
the opposing king to a file or rank along the edge by closing off
escape paths, while your king marches down and herds the prey
into a corner.

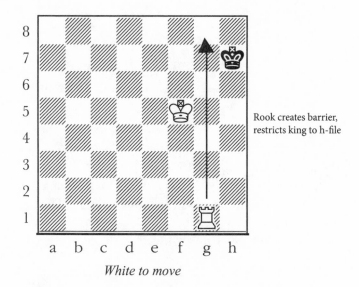

Rook creates barrier,
restricts king to h-file

White to move

Up to now, the White rook has been used primarily to keep
Black's king on the last file.

Rg6. Now White brings the rook down to g6, where he is protected from capture by his king, cutting off the h6 square.

Black's only move is to the corner (h8).

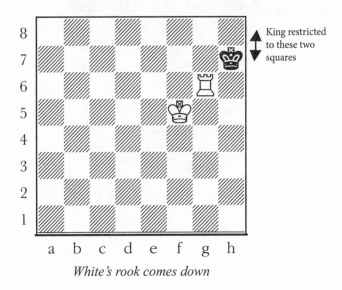

White's rook comes down

White pushes his king to f6 and Black returns to h7, the only square he can legally go to. White's king advances again, to f7. Black, with no other possible moves, returns back to the corner.

Now it's time. Do you see the checkmate?

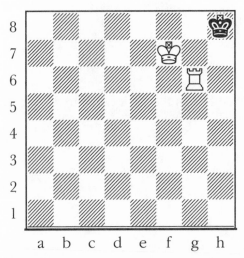

White to move—do you see the checkmate?

White cannot move the rook to g8, because it will allow Black's king to escape to h7 and beyond, away from the corner where White wants him. Moving the rook to g7 would be a big mistake, as we'll see in a minute. There is a better move, a decisive one.

Rh6 checkmate. White's king blocks off the escape route while the rook delivers the final blow.

Rh6 checkmate!

Endgame Danger—Stalemate

You have a stalemate when the only possible move for a player not currently in check is a move *into* check. This is why you don't make the move Rg7 in the above game. Instead of a checkmate, White would have unintentionally forced a stalemate. The game would be drawn, much to Black's satisfaction and White's bitter disappointment.

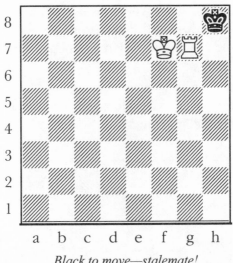

Black to move—stalemate!

6. ENDGAME MATE WITH A QUEEN

If you arrive at the endgame with a queen and a king versus your opponent's king, victory is in hand and you just need to close it down. It doesn't matter if there are some extra pawns scattered around for both you and your opponent—the same checkmating strategies apply.

Just be careful—don't let your opponent promote a pawn into a queen and don't maneuver yourself into a stalemate.

The queen cannot mate your opponent's king by itself. Like the rook-and-king mate, the queen will need an assist from the king.

Your strategy is the same: Herd the king to the edge of the board and finish him off with the queen.

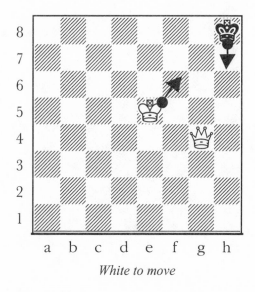

White to move

White's queen has cut off the board, forming an invisible barrier on the g-file that his opponent cannot cross—the Black king's movement is limited to the h-file. White's king heads toward the killing zone. A few moves earlier, the king was on c3, but he continues his progress across the board. The queen will need its protection for the final play.

White to move.

Kf6. White's king is in route toward Black's king. He is close, the end is coming soon.

...Kh7. The Black king makes his only legal move, from h8 to h7. It is too late for anything but to wait for White to end it. His only hope is a blunder that either leaves White's queen hanging or forces a stalemate.

White's king on f6 is now in range for the assist.

Do you see the checkmate?

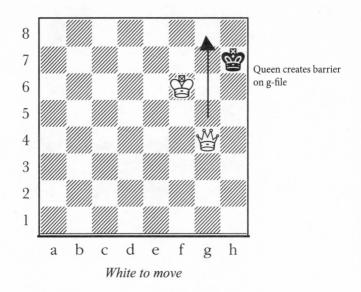

Queen creates barrier on g-file

White to move

And now White finishes the job: **Qg7 checkmate.**

The deed is done—checkmate!

7. ENDGAME MATE WITH A KNIGHT OR BISHOP

With just a king and knight, or a king and bishop against a lone king, checkmate is not possible. You have a drawn game. If you're the player up a piece, you must preserve a pawn well before the endgame so it can, hopefully, be promoted to a queen and a won game—otherwise you have wasted your advantage and turned a won game into a draw.

Let's say you have a knight and a king against an opponent with a bishop, pawn and king, and have the opportunity to exchange your knight for his bishop or his pawn. Choose the pawn! With just a bishop and king, he cannot win. However, he *can* win with a pawn and the king by promoting the pawn to a queen, a combination that can very much checkmate your king. We'll see how to turn a pawn into a win in our next position.

8. ENDGAME PAWN PROMOTION

The lowly pawn becomes a powerful piece in the endgame because it poses the threat of promoting to a queen. And that is exactly what Black is trying to do here.

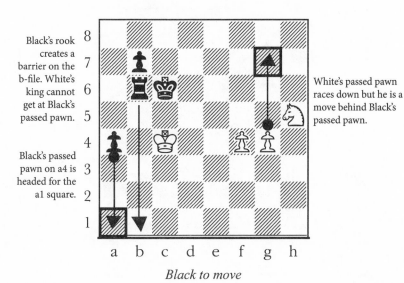

Black's rook creates a barrier on the b-file. White's king cannot get at Black's passed pawn.

White's passed pawn races down but he is a move behind Black's passed pawn.

Black's passed pawn on a4 is headed for the a1 square.

Black to move

Black has a passed pawn on a4 and the only piece that can stop it is White's king—except he can't. Black's rook has created a barrier on the b-file over which White's king cannot cross. White's knight is too far away and there is nothing that can be done to stop the pawn's progress. White, in a desperate attempt to salvage this game, races his own pawns down the other side of the board with hopes of queening, but he is a step behind Black in the race. Here is how it plays out.

37. ---	**a3**
38. g5	**a2**
39. g6	**a1=Q**
40. g7	

The pawns race down in opposite directions and down opposite sides of the board. Black has now made it all the way down to a1 and promoted to a queen. White gets as far as g7, one square away from his own promotion.

So close, but yet so far!

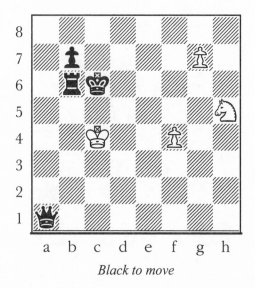

Black to move

From here, Black makes quick work of White, cutting off the
ranks toward a destined fate. First, a check on White's king by
moving the newly promoted queen to a4, then a check from the
rook moving to b3.

| ... | Qa4+ |
| Kd3 | Rb3 |

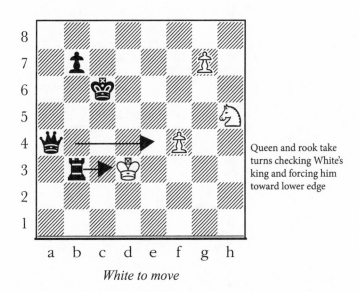

Queen and rook take
turns checking White's
king and forcing him
toward lower edge

White to move

We saw a similar mate earlier in this chapter (mating with two
rooks). You just keep cutting off the board with the queen and
rook combo, putting the opposing king into check and forcing
him toward the edge until there is no place left to hide.

Two more moves and the dirty deed will be done. Queen to the
second rank (a2 square), then rook to the first rank (b1 square),
and then it will all be over.

9. SNEAKY MATE

Here is one final game situation. Black has just moved and it is White's turn.

Do you see White's unstoppable checkmate?

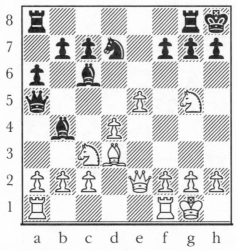

White to move. Do you see the unstoppable mate?

Bam! **Nxf7** checkmate!

All these pieces on the board, yet White's knight, all by his lonesome, checkmates the king. Marvelous!

Bam! Game over!

12. HOW TO SAVE LOST GAMES

A lost game occurs when a player faces a material disadvantage seemingly too difficult to overcome and rendering his chances to win highly unlikely. However, among beginners, who have limited board vision and are prone to terrible blunders, a game is never truly lost until the final bell is rung and the losing player has been checkmated. Anything can happen in the interim—and we've seen many examples of that in this book—so no matter how dire the situation, just remember the mantra, "It ain't over until it's over."

Make your opponent checkmate you. Don't give up. There is hope and here is the well from which you can draw some...

1. LOOK FOR A TRICKY CHECKMATE

Your best hope for saving a lost game is to position yourself for a daring checkmate. You line up pieces for a mating attack while allowing your opponent to grab meaningless material. By slowly maneuvering your pieces into a deadly formation, you can surprise a distracted pawn-snatching opponent with a sudden mate he should have seen coming—but never did.

In the following game, that is exactly White's plan.

Watch how he forces the action and distracts Black while getting ready to pounce.

A Lost Game is Saved!

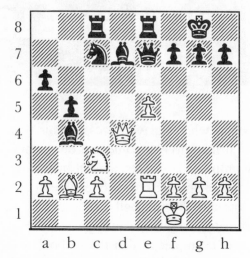

White has a lost game—but hope. White to move

White is in deep trouble, down a rook and a knight, which is an insurmountable disadvantage against a competent player. The game would be resigned at higher levels of play. But at the beginning levels; let's not rush to judgment!

White does have an extra pawn, but that is entirely meaningless in the context of a two-piece disadvantage. What is not meaningless is that White has a plan. He sees a potential mate and just needs a few moves to get his pieces in position. Meanwhile, Black is seriously coiled up with a massive arsenal pointed in the direction of White's king, and there is not a lot of time to work with.

White must act fast and decisively. Where there is life, there is hope, and White thinks he has some hope.

23. Nd5. White's knight advances to the d5 square. It's a triple fork, simultaneously attacking Black's bishop (on b4), knight (on c7) and queen (on e7). Black sees the threats, but is unconcerned. He can simply capture White's knight (an even exchange since White can capture back with the queen), with the side benefit of opening up the c-file for his rook.

23...Nxd5. There is not much to think about here. Black captures the White knight, giving White one less piece to work with. Black expects White to capture back with his queen, but that's perfectly fine—exchanging pieces is a good plan when ahead.

23. e6. White pushes his e-pawn up a square, attacking Black's bishop on d7.

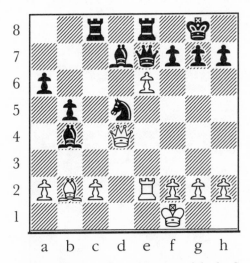

Can White pull a rabbit out of the hat?

Black stares at the move for a moment. He is surprised White didn't take his knight and complete the exchange. He exclaims silently to himself—what is White thinking? Has White just blundered away *another* piece? Black is bothered by White's attacking pawn and wants it removed. Left alone, it will either take Black's bishop at d7 or his pawn at f7, giving check to the king and exposing his queen to a discovered attack by White's e2 rook. A clever little play if Black sleeps on the discovered check. Black is certainly not going to take the pawn directly with his queen and lose it to that same rook.

Black could also take White's offending pawn with his f7 pawn, but he doesn't want to weaken his kingside protection or block his rook and queen, which are powerfully lined up on the e-file, pointed in the direction of a potential back rank mate. But Black prefers another option, capturing the e6 pawn with his bishop.

23... Bxe6. Black jumps at the chance to pile on and take another piece, even if it's a lowly pawn left hanging on e6 like a sitting duck. Black is only too happy to pull out his hunting rifle and bring it down with the bishop. Not only that, the bishop now protects the knight at d5, meaning White's queen can no longer take the knight and complete the exchange.

Black now has a three piece advantage!

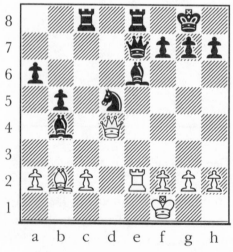

Black's bishop takes the e6 pawn

Black is thrilled to grab free material two turns in a row. The rout is on. Now he's up a rook and two knights, he has evened the pawns, and his pieces are lined up for an imminent attack. A slaughter! Black is very pleased with the way the game is going. A slight smirk accompanies Black's last move. His material edge, along with his ego, is growing.

But there won't be a next move. White has a surprise in store.

24. Qxg1 mate!

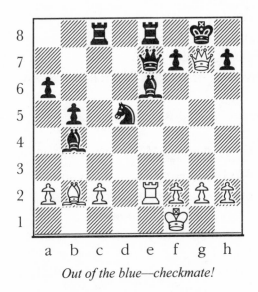

Out of the blue—checkmate!

What the heck?

White came from nowhere with this brilliantly disguised checkmate. White cleverly made his knight move first—it was important to eliminate Black's knight as a potential capturing piece on the subsequent e6 pawn move White was going to make. That knight would then protect the g7 space White was targeting for the mate. That possibility was removed when White enticed the Black knight to take his own knight at d5, a gift Black was only too happy to accept.

Then White got Black to bite again at his advancing e6 pawn.

Had Black captured with his f7 pawn, the attack would have been defused as Black's queen would now have an open line to defend the vulnerable g7 pawn. But Black never considered the sneaky mate White had lined up so it was not even a thought. He was too busy adding to his collection of captured pieces. And Black's knight, as we just discussed, was no longer in position to take the e6 pawn. That left the bishop as the most logical piece if Black took the bait, which indeed he did.

Meanwhile, White kept Black busy capturing pieces while his real intent was disguised—removing pieces on the black diagonal so that his queen and bishop could have an unobstructed attack to deliver the final blow. Black never saw what hit him.

White's plan worked. A lost game was saved!

2. LOOK FOR A DRAW

When you're so hopelessly beaten that you need a Hail Mary, sometimes your best strategy at salvation is to maneuver for a draw through perpetual check (or hope your opponent blunders into a stalemate). Below White cooked up a perpetual check:

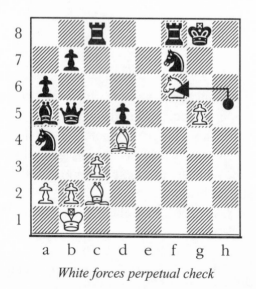

White forces perpetual check

White has maneuvered into a position where he can perpetually check his opponent and Black can do nothing about it. In the diagram above, White had just moved his knight from the e5 square to f6 putting Black's king in check. The king's only escape square is g7.

White's knight now continues to e8!

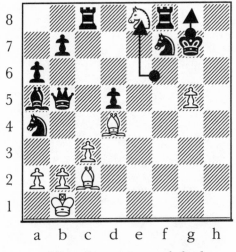

White forces perpetual check

This creates a discovered check by White's d4 bishop along with a simultaneous second check with the knight. Black can do nothing but return to g8. White's knight returns to f6, the same position as before—check. This move order, like a skipping indestructible record, can repeat itself over and over again until eternity—it is perpetual check.

So despite White having an overwhelming advantage *and* an imminent mate, he has to settle for a draw!

Another lost game was saved!

3. LOOK FOR WAYS TO PROMOTE

You can sometimes salvage a lost game by sneaking a pawn all the way down the board to the point where your opponent can no longer halt its progress. Promoting a queen into your army is a huge game changer, perhaps enough to turn the game around.

13. SPEED CHESS

A super fun version of the standard game is called *speed chess*. Rather than the normal chess game where moves are made at your leisure, in speed chess you have a limited amount of time to make *all* your moves. The typical time limit for each side is five minutes, though you can set the game time to any amount agreed upon by the players.

There are two rules for speed chess that differ from standard chess:

1. **If you run out of time, you lose.** It doesn't matter if you're up a queen and two rooks and are just one move from mating your opponent. If your time runs out, you lose—but only if your opponent notices that you're out of time! If he sleeps on it, you can still win by checkmating him before he discovers your time ran out.

2. **You can take off your opponent's king if he fails to protect it.** Checking is not announced in speed chess. If an opponent overlooks your check and makes a different move, for example, taking your queen, you simply take off his king—game over!

The time limit and the ability to remove the king, added to the pressure of precious little time to complete your entire game, makes speed chess exciting. Victory can get snatched from the jaws of defeat by an overlooked check or the precipitous dagger of the clock. Speed of play and the ability to think under pressure are paramount. You can't think too much in speed chess. You need to move and move fast. This leads to games with the most ridiculous blunders and with players overlooking them as well!

To play five-minute chess, you need a chess clock, which is actually two clocks built into the same plastic or wooden housing—one clock for each player. The chess clock sits between the players on the table, next to the board. After completing a move, you press down the button on your side of the chess clock. This will stop your clock and activate your opponent's clock. Time ticks away on his clock until he moves and depresses his clock's button, which starts your clock and stops his own.

One more rule to keep in mind in speed chess is that you have to hit the clock with the same hand that you use to move the pieces. So if you make a move with your right hand, the right hand must also be used to press the clock's button.

Let's say both you and your opponent have used up three minutes of time after twenty moves. On the 21st move, the situation gets complicated and your opponent eats up thirty seconds on his clock. You quickly respond with a further complicating move. He goes back into the tank for another thirty seconds. Now he has a total of only one minute to complete the entire game giving you a sizable advantage. He'll have to move fast for the remainder of the game so that he doesn't run out of time.

Handicapping by Time

You can equalize players of unequal skills by assigning a time handicap. I used to play speed chess with my ex-girlfriend and handicapped the match by giving myself one minute to her full five minutes. I was a stronger player so that put the game on more equal footing. Needless to say, it was a frantic pace for me.

I got really good at playing fast to a degree that surprised me. It took a trip to New York City and a match against professional hustlers before I realized I had become a speed-chess monster.

14. AVERY VERSUS THE NEW YORK CITY STREET HUSTLERS

On a visit to Washington Square Park in New York City, legendary home to hustlers adept at five-minute chess, my ex, who overrated my chess-playing abilities, urged me to take on the hustlers for a little fun. I knew that these hustlers were phenomenal players—that's what they did for a living—and I didn't think I could play with them. Speed chess encompasses other skills that excellent players accustomed to standard time-limit chess don't possess in equal portions, so that when the twain meet, the hustlers typically prevail due to their proficiency in the speed version of the game.

I was no match for the hustlers, but my ex insisted, fully confident I could beat them. In addition, I knew she loved listening to me trash talk, as I did in our home poker games, and she wanted to watch me in action against the hustlers. She wasn't aware of the many levels in the hierarchy of chess skills and that these guys, in speed chess, were near the top.

One of the players saw me hesitate in front of a table and beckoned me over. "What the heck," I said to myself, "might as well." Better than being peppered to death by the ex. I took a seat on the concrete bench across the board from him and prepared for battle. He told me it was $20 for the game, winner takes all.

"Okay," I said, "let's get it on."

There was some pre-game razzing, warm-ups so to speak, but not too much from me *yet*—I was going to let my chess pieces do the talking if, indeed, they could. I didn't want to open my mouth too much if I couldn't back it up.

The game began like a dizzying whirlwind. I was really fast and played such an aggressive opening that, not too many moves in, my opponent soon saw he had more than his hands full. I was no ordinary park challenger. I was accustomed to one minute games and played with a speed and dynamic style that rocked him like a boxer's haymaker. After I took him out, he realized he was no match for me. I was done letting my chess pieces do the talking. I was having fun and let my mouth have its turn. He was outclassed and I let him know that.

I might have been having fun, but he and his buddies at the park weren't. The hustlers were accustomed to taking money, not giving it. They weren't there as a street charity for the passersby, they were the receptacles of such contributions. The money was going in the wrong direction and my opponent didn't like it one bit. I took his $20 bill, turned it over a few times, and then gave it a long exaggerated sniff. Oh yeah, it smelled good. Word got around and another hustler, a better player presumably, sauntered over from a neighboring table. Someone needed to set the record straight and shut me up.

Only he didn't either.

I wiped him and his street talk off the board. *And took his $20.* And gave that bill an exaggerated sniff as well. I had to rub it in. That's what you do in the city.

This was war now. The hustlers, all of whom were black with a good sense of city humor—when they were winning, at least—

were plenty riled up. The white guy with the big mouth needed to be put in his place, and their money needed to be won back. My initial victim exited the area and returned thirty seconds later with the best player in the park—the king hustler.

"How about we play for $60, the original $40 you got, and another $20 on top of that?" he said. "What do you say, brother?"

"Rock and roll," I said, "let's see what you got. Hopefully it's a little something more than your buddies, I'm tired of playing preschoolers. I need a little challenge here, my man."

"We'll see, brother."

We got the preliminaries out of the way, thirty seconds of trash talking while we set up the pieces and he set the clock. I got White, the customary color given to the challengers. I'd go first.

He hit my button, starting my clock, and the game began. The king soon saw that I wasn't a cupcake.. My ultra-aggressive opening and lightning fast moves quickly put the king hustler on the defensive. After ten moves, I had the edge and we raced into the middle game.

All talk had stopped. This was war on the chessboard. After an aggressive move which took off a piece, I slammed his captured piece on the clock's button, an act of chess arrogance, and exclaimed, "One down!" The king only glanced at me, but my brashness registered. He captured back, evening the exchange, but I was making sure he knew this was psychological warfare and guerilla tactics.

And then, "Two down!" I screamed, when another piece of his left the game, accompanied by another arrogant slam of his captured piece on the table. He captured an equivalent piece of mine on his next move, keeping the material about even.

The king hustler was a better player than me—I think all the guys at this park were—but I had speed like he hadn't encountered before and a tough, dynamic opening that gave him trouble under the time pressure. I was accustomed to playing one-minute blitzkrieg chess, so to me, five minutes was an eternity. I could play really fast. My time advantage grew as he wrestled with the complications on the board.

He too was fast with his moves, but not like me. I was "The Flash" and my speed of play put extreme pressure on him.

The king hustler's superior skills started to play out and tilt the game in his favor. He got up a piece and had a better position, but it came at an exorbitant cost against my furious unfamiliar attack—time, sweet precious time, an exchange I was very happy to make. In fact, that was my game strategy anyway—to move so fast that when he thought, it was always on his time and not mine, even at the cost of some disadvantages. In a regular game, the ending would have been a foregone conclusion and I would have resigned. But this was speed chess and the king had paid too steep a price for his deliberations. The king's clock had about run out—he was down to but a mere few seconds. He had maybe one move's worth of time left, two at the most.

The speed of The Flash was carrying the day.

A quick glance at the king hustler's buddies was satisfying. They had crowded around the table watching The Flash take on their king. Their chatter and jawing at the beginning of the game had turned to silence and concerned expressions—the king was in trouble, and him and his $60 might be going down!

I was at the cusp of victory. Any move I chose to make, no matter how ridiculous, would lead to a win—except the move I ignored. The king hustler had put me in check with a sneaky bishop advance that I slept on. I got sidetracked by my own tangent and foolishly never even looked at his move, a common fault I warn about in this book. There was plenty of time left on my clock and I should have used a few seconds of it to consider his move. But I was too wound up pressuring him and didn't want to give him any of my time to think.

I quickly moved, hit the clock, and with a smile my opponent couldn't contain, he whipped off my king. The king's flag fell immediately afterwards, indicating he ran out of time, but it was too late. The game was already over. The king had won.

I had the king hustler right where I wanted him, moments away from defeat, but I didn't take the few seconds I needed to consider his move and, as a result, fell to his capture of my king. And that was that. Live by the sword, die by the sword.

The king hustler got all the other hustlers' money back and an extra $20 besides. It was a great game and we shook hands with gusto. The king hustler knew he pulled a rabbit out of his hat— he had a lost game—but he appreciated the speed and skills of The Flash. It was an exciting, hard fought game, whose fortunes turned on the last few seconds. The king had salvaged the hustler's bruised egos and won back their losses—an important dual victory for the hustlers at Washington Square Park. It was a good victory for me as well. I had outplayed the hustlers and had their king on the ropes.

The king wanted to go at me again, but I think he was relieved when I passed on it. He knew that a rematch against The Flash would be tough. Anyway, it was time for lunch, and a bite at Mamoun's on MacDougal Street in the East Village beckoned.

A good falafel lunch was calling and there was nothing I could do but answer that call.

15. TOURNAMENT CHESS & RATINGS

TOURNAMENT CHESS

If you become serious about playing chess, you might consider joining a local chess club where you can compete and fraternize with like-minded individuals, and perhaps enter chess tournaments, which are a lot of fun. Tournaments give you a chance to compete against other chess players in a great setting with an opportunity to win trophies and often cash prizes if you do really well.

In tournaments, scores are kept by wins, losses, and draws. You get 1 point for a win, 1/2 point for a draw, and 0 points for a loss. So if you were to play 11 games in a tournament, won seven, drew one, and lost three games, you would have earned 7½ points, finishing ahead of players with fewer points and, of course, behind players with more.

In tournaments, you will be matched against players of similar skill levels. Also, sometime after the conclusion of the tournament, you'll be assigned a chess rating, which will be posted on the chess federation's website (new.uschess.org/home). In the United States, the USCF is the national federation that keeps track of ratings.

Outside of the United States, FIDE (www.FIDE.com) is the ruling body in the chess world. FIDE maintains its own set of ratings, similar to the USCF ratings.

CHESS RATINGS

Chess ratings are a measure of a chess player's ability; the higher the rating, the greater a chess player's skill level. Ratings are derived from your performance against other rated players. Wins will earn you a certain number of points—the higher your opponent's rating, the more points you'll earn—while losses will deduct points by a similar methodology. Similarly, draws against better players get you points, and against weaker players, lose you points.

As you get more experience and become a better player, your ratings will rise. In the chess world, ratings define a player's strength. For example, a player with a chess rating of 1800 is considerably stronger than a player rated around 1600 and, by the same token, significantly weaker than a player holding a chess rating of 2000. A victory against an opponent with a rating 200 points higher than your own would be an upset. A 100-point rating gap indicates a smaller gap in skills between players, while a 400-point differential is a huge mismatch.

Ratings 1200 or below indicate a beginning-level player, with the lower the rating, the weaker the player, while ratings of 1200 to 1600 might be considered an intermediate player. When a player is rated above 1600, to about 1800, he is an advanced intermediate player. While an 1800 rated player is about four skill levels below being a threat among world-class players, he would also be almost unbeatable among casual players. Players rated 2000 and even 2200 are amazing players, but even there, they're nowhere close to the very best in the world of chess. So, as you see, there is a very distinct hierarchy in the skill levels among chess players.

The top levels of players in the world are called *grandmasters*. Their ratings are about 2400-2500 (and over) with the very best, the *Super Grandmasters*, holding ratings 2700 and higher.

Magnus Carlsen, the World Chess Champion from Norway, reached the highest ranking ever, at 2882 in 2014.

Ratings vary every time you compete in a tournament so you'll get a lot of enjoyment watching your ratings progress. It's great fun to watch your chess ratings bump higher after a successful tournament, or even grow by leaps and bounds after a hugely successful showing. If you keep improving your play, your chess ratings will go with it, and you'll start climbing the ladder of success in the chess world.

Below is a list of the USCF ratings levels.

USCF Ratings

Class J	100-199
Class I	200-399
Class H	400-599
Class G	600-799
Class F	800-999
Class E	1100-1199
Class D	1200-1399
Class C	1400-1599
Class B	1600-1799
Class A	1800-1999
Expert	2100-2399
International Master	2200-2399
Senior Master	2400 +

THE LAST WORD

We're covered a lot of ground and I hope *Chess ASAP!* has given you a good understanding of how to play and how to win at the wonderful pastime of chess, plus a genuine feeling of excitement for the game.

There is so much more to learn about chess and you'll really have a great time on this lifelong journey. If you keep working at improving your skills—through buying quality chess books, playing games, and competing in tournaments—you will get better and better!

Hey, I don't want to keep you any longer. We've had a really nice walk in the world of chess and hopefully this door has opened up a new world for you in this great adventure.

I wish you great enjoyment and great skill at chess!